WINNING
THROUGH
INTIMIDATION

WINNING
THROUGH
INTIMIDATION

How to Be the Victor,
Not the Victim,
in Business and in Life

By

Robert Ringer

SKYHORSE PUBLISHING

Skyhorse Publishing books may be purchased in bulk at special discounts for sales promotion, corporate gifts, fund-raising, or educational purposes. Special editions can also be created to specifications. For details, contact the Special Sales Department, Skyhorse Publishing, 307 West 36th Street, 11th Floor, New York, NY 10018 or info@skyhorsepublishing.com.

Skyhorse® and Skyhorse Publishing® are registered trademarks of Skyhorse Publishing, Inc.®, a Delaware corporation.

www.skyhorsepublishing.com

10 9 8 7

Library of Congress Cataloging-in-Publication Data is available on file.

ISBN: 978-1-62636-114-0

Printed in the United States of America

Dedicated to the millions of resilient souls who took to heart Peter Finch's battle cry in the movie *Network*—"We're mad as hell, and we're not going to take it anymore!"—by adopting it as their mantra and drawing a line in the sand against the intimidators of the world.

Contents

PREFACE

Notwithstanding its rise to *New York Times* #1 bestseller status, the title of this book, *Winning Through Intimidation*, sparked a great deal of controversy over the years. I was often made aware of the fact that many people refused to read the book because they assumed it was about bullying your way to the top. For this very reason, many other people—those who actually read the book—insisted that it was mistitled, because it was not, as the title seemed to suggest, a tome on how to get ahead by intimidating others.

As a result, for a number of years the title was changed to *To Be or Not to Be Intimidated?* And that, in turn, caused many readers to register complaints and adamantly state that they preferred the original title because it was more bold. So, I guess it's true that everything that goes around comes around, and here we are again, back to the original title. In any event, just to be clear, *Winning Through Intimidation* and *To Be or Not to Be Intimidated?* are one and the same.

That said, if you bought this book in the hopes that it might teach you how to get ahead in life by intimidating others, I'm afraid you've made a bad choice. If that's your aim, you might find *The Communist Manifesto, Mein Kampf,* or *Mao Tse-Tung on Guerrilla Warfare* more to your liking. As you will see on the following pages, *Winning Through Intimidation* is a guide to *defending* yourself *against* intimidating people.

Be forewarned: More often than not, those who feign indignation over the mere mention of the word *intimidation* are the very people who are most likely to use it against you. So, make no mistake about it, what I have to say in this book bothers a lot of people—especially self-righteous, self-anointed saints who are masters at intimidating others. They would prefer that most people not understand that intimidation is a common thread that runs through every business situation and a crucial factor that decides the outcome of many of life's most important events.

At the top of the list of master intimidators disguised as (self-anointed) saints are chest-pounding critics, syndicated columnists, and TV commentators, ever on the alert for an opportunity to seize the moral high ground. Like public figures in all fields of endeavor, authors find it an annoying challenge to fend off their intimidating mischaracterizations and misleading comments.

What is a tortoise to do about such a relentless onslaught of distortion and truth-twisting, of having to listen to "the truth you've spoken twisted by knaves to make a trap for fools?" Ayn Rand offered perhaps the most rational solution for dealing with slanderers when she said, "Freedom comes from seeing the ignorance of your critics and discovering the emptiness of their virtue." Thankfully, I long ago adopted her advice, and highly recommend that you do the same with regard to those who would try to misrepresent your words or actions.

INTRODUCTION

The principles set forth on the following pages do not necessarily represent the way I or anyone else may *wish* the world to be, but the way it actually *is*. In other words, it is a work based on reality, particularly as it relates to human nature. Thus, the essence of the philosophy contained herein should serve you well regardless of how the world around you may change in the years ahead.

That's because, though technology continually changes, human nature remains constant. People, by and large, are pretty much the same today as they were in the times of Confucius, Buddha, Jesus, and Socrates, and it's a safe bet that they'll be pretty much the same 2,000 years from now. For example, Jesus, above all else, crusaded against hypocrisy. But today, 2,000 years later, can anyone seriously say they see evidence that hypocrisy is on the decline?

Judging from the way most people talk and act, one is led to wonder if a resistance to reality is genetically programmed into a majority of our species. Perhaps reality was only meant to be embraced elsewhere in our universe. However, unless you know how to build a spaceship—and fly it—I would suggest that it would be much easier for you to join that small minority of people on Planet Earth who are vigilant when it comes to recognizing and acknowledging reality.

Unfortunately, most people choose to live in a world of delusions, stubbornly refusing to accept the unforgiving realities of life no matter how great the evidence to support such realities may be. Why? Because truth is often painful, and people simply do not like pain. My position, however, is that truth, by its very nature, is always preferable to falsehood, regardless of how unpleasant it may be. Self-delusion leads to certain failure, and failure leads to misery. What's so noble about promoting misery?

Sure, I sometimes think to myself that perhaps it would be easier to yield to the temptation to become an ostrich and simply hide my head in the sands of unreality. In the end, though, I always manage to pull myself back toward reality, because I'd rather go to my grave a battered realist than a bloodied ostrich. And rest assured that battering *is* an integral part of the journey— no matter who you are or what you choose to believe.

As you will see, to a great extent this book is an autobiographical work centered around my years as a real estate broker. However, subsequent events have repeatedly demonstrated to my satisfaction that the lessons learned during my years in the real estate business apply not only to all other kinds of business endeavors, but to virtually all other aspects of life as well. Unfortunately, anyone who misses this central point misses the book.

Finally, a warning. The following pages are not suitable for weak stomachs. The painful tales that lie ahead may cause you to recall equally unpleasant experiences from your own life. With that caveat, I suggest that you lock away all sharp objects and place the Pepto-Bismol within easy reach before beginning Chapter 1.

CHAPTER 1

SHATTERING THE MYTHS

The overriding message in many motivation and personal-development books is that if a person just maintains a positive mental attitude and works long, hard hours, he will ultimately succeed. A nice thought, to be sure, but one that borders more on mysticism than reality.

How many times have you seen a person get all charged up after reading a motivation book, then, after the initial high wears off, become more frustrated than ever when he* realizes that he is no closer to achieving his goals than before reading the book?

---

*Because I find it cumbersome to use hybrid pronouns such as "his/hers," and am opposed to debasing the English language by mixing singular nouns and pronouns with plural pronouns such as "they," I have, for convenience only, chosen to use the masculine gender throughout this book in most instances where the neuter has not been employed.

Perhaps it's even happened to you. To be sure, I experienced this phenomenon many times earlier in my career.

There's no question that the illusions created by the hyperbole and dynamic verbiage contained in many motivation and personal-development books can be very uplifting, but almost without exception they fail to address the realities that confront a person when he ventures into the Business World Jungle and comes face to face with its indigenous predators.

When these face-to-face confrontations occur, the synthetically motivated individual becomes confused and frustrated when discovering, to his dismay, that Jungle predators don't have a whole lot of interest in his positive mental attitude or work ethic. Unfortunately, this harsh reality often causes the individual to cling to his favorite motivation author's assurances that ultimately success will come if he just toughs it out and adheres to some simple rules. Sort of like waiting for one's reward in the afterlife.

Like millions of other people, I, too, fell into the trap of believing that my great reward would ultimately come if I just focused on working hard and displaying a positive mental attitude. However, my rewards did not come until I invested a great deal of time and thought into carefully analyzing my frustrating failures of the past and developing the courage to allow truth and logic to prevail.

The turning point for me came one day when I was having a discussion with a financially successful acquaintance of mine ("Vern") who headed up his own insurance agency. Vern had always intrigued me, because, outwardly, he seemed like the world's least likely candidate to become a success at anything, let alone selling. He was quiet to the point of being shy, and was very awkward in his mannerisms. In addition, he gave no outward indication of harboring a positive mental attitude, and worked fewer hours than anyone I had ever known.

Vern's success shattered the archetypal image of the "super salesman" that I had held in my mind from the time I was a youngster. It helped me to better understand why so many individuals whom others had characterized as great salesmen often lacked the results to back up their reputations. I now realize that when someone is tagged as a "great salesman," all too often it's the very reason why he is *not* successful at his craft. The problem is that the individual with a mega-reputation as a super salesman poses a threat to a prospect the moment he enters the room. Over a period of time, I developed a knack for spotting these paper-tiger salesmen, and came to refer to them fondly as the "all show, no dough" brigade; i.e., they were more successful in attracting attention than getting results.

During one of my conversations with Vern, I pointed out that the methods espoused in many so-called success books did not seem to work in actual practice, and asked his opinion as to why. His answer was quite surprising. Vern explained that successful people rarely know the real reasons for their success, though they themselves almost always *believe* that they know. When I expressed my curiosity as to why a person would be unaware of how he had achieved his own success, he said it was a matter of a person being too close to the trees of his business to see the forest of his success. Absolutely fascinating insight, and one that I have never forgotten.

With Vern's intriguing observation in mind, I came to the conclusion, over a period of time, that there were a number of reasons why successful people, as well as the authors of so many self-help books, tend to espouse unworkable solutions. These include, among others:

- Success has a tendency to breed self-righteousness, which all too often causes a person to overemphasize, to the exclusion of other crucial factors, such societal favorites as positive mental attitude and work ethic.

- The media, government, and academia are relentless in their intimidating efforts to try to make financially successful people feel guilty. As a result, those at the high end of the financial spectrum are often self-conscious about their wealth and tend to repress the realities of how they achieved it. More to the point, they are concerned about little inconveniences such as being burned at the stake by the envious masses.

- Finally, many authors of business, personal-development, and motivation books deliberately withhold, for commercial reasons, the realities of what it takes to succeed. It's much easier, and far more popular, to sell success myths that people have been weaned on since their earliest days in grade school than to say things that are certain to incur the wrath of society's absolute moralists—those who roam the earth searching for perceived bad guys. Aspiring authors of self-help books quickly learn to heed Publishing Rule Number One: *Reality is a hard sell.* Shooting truth messengers is considered a noble occupation in a Western culture turned upside down.

I want to make it clear that, notwithstanding anything I have said up to this point, there is no question in my mind that both a positive mental attitude and a good work ethic are important to an individual's success. The problem arises when one relies *solely* on these two virtues to the exclusion of all other factors. Having a positive mental attitude and a good work ethic are two traits that are so often misunderstood that I feel it is important to discuss them in more detail before moving on.

Positive Mental Attitude. It has been my observation that most people have a distorted concept of what constitutes a true positive mental attitude. "Just fake it till you make it" are perhaps the most damaging motivational words ever spoken, yet I've heard this phrase repeated by positive mental attitude enthusiasts many times over the years.

In reality, you can't acquire a positive mental attitude simply by standing in front of a mirror and reciting self-energizing slogans, force-feeding your mind with positive thoughts, or heartily shaking people's hands (while grinning from ear to ear) and loudly exclaiming, "Great!" when someone asks you how things are going.

By contrast, a *real* positive mental attitude can play a major role in one's success, but such an attitude is a *result* of being prepared. In other words, a true positive mental attitude is possible only through one's having the ammunition to back it up. You develop a positive mental attitude by being good at what you do, by understanding the realities of what it takes to succeed, and by having the self-discipline to base your actions on those realities.

The success cycle is self-perpetuating: The more prepared a person is, the more confident he becomes, which translates into a *natural* positive mental attitude, which in turn increases his chances of success. You can set all the goals you want, but I can guarantee that you won't achieve them if you're not prepared. Preparation and a positive mental attitude work in concert to help you achieve your goals.

But even after I concluded that a positive mental attitude was not a quality that anyone could synthesize, I still found myself venturing into the Business World Jungle (specifically, at that point in time, the real estate brokerage area of the Jungle), sincerely believing that, because of my preparation, I would succeed in closing every deal, only to end up having my head handed to me on a platter because of realities over which I had little or no control. As I struck out on one sale after another, it became clear to me that it was just a matter of time until my self-esteem—and my self-confidence along with it—was shattered. The result was confusion and doubt.

Then, at some point in time, it occurred to me that even though I possessed a reasonable amount of self-confidence and was well prepared, I still was lacking a method for *sustaining* my positive mental attitude in the face of repeated disappointments. This evolved into one of my earliest theories, and prompted a major shift upward in my career.

What I am referring to is the **Theory of Next**, which states: *The key to maintaining a positive mental attitude is to recognize* *that no one deal is that important. The person with a true positive mental attitude possesses the power to say "Next!" and quickly move on to the next deal when things don't work out.*

The reason it's okay if a deal falls through is because day-to-day "failure" is an integral part of long-term success. So, part and parcel to a true positive mental attitude is having the mental toughness to move quickly on to the next deal when a deal you've been working on blows up. Anticipating continual short-term setbacks has the positive effect of deflating their impact on your mental state when they occur, which in turn paves the way for long-term success.

This realistic approach to life simply takes into account circumstances beyond one's control, but PMA one-trick ponies seem totally incapable of grasping this obvious fact of life. If you still have a pulse rate and are over twenty-one years of age, surely personal experience has demonstrated to you that no matter how well prepared you are, most situations in life don't work out as planned. In real estate, for example, a deal can blow up over any one of a seemingly infinite number of unforeseen obstacles—e.g., unwanted third-party opinions, ulterior motives on the part of the buyer or seller, or even a change in the health or marital status of one of the parties.

Consequently, I ultimately concluded that the only way to guard against having my self-confidence and belief shattered was to acknowledge the reality that, like it or not, most deals do not close. I reasoned that the only way I could sustain a true positive mental attitude was to come to grips with this reality and make certain that I was always mentally prepared to move on to the next deal.

Did it work? Spectacularly. My income skyrocketed during the first year that I implemented the Theory of Next, but it's important to point out that the deals I closed during that year represented only a small fraction of the total number of deals I worked on. In essence, I simply accessed the power of the law of averages. Also, it's noteworthy to point out that I worked just as hard, and in many instances harder, on the scores of deals that *didn't* close as I did on the ones that resulted in big payoffs. Given these realities, there is no question in my mind that without my firm belief in the Theory of Next, I would not have had the confidence and persistence to press on after seeing one sale after another go up in smoke.

I guess you might say that it was a paradox of sorts in that I prepared for long-term success by bracing myself against the effects of short-term failure. I again emphasize that this philosophy works only if you are *prepared* to succeed. It does not work if you simply use it as an excuse to fail in a situation where it may have been possible to succeed had you tried harder or been more persistent.

With this unorthodox perspective indelibly stamped on my forebrain, I was able to view each negative result as a learning experience and studiously focus on extracting the lessons learned from each experience. Then, of utmost importance, I simply deleted the negative result from my mind. When it comes to situations that don't work out, whether in my business or personal life, my motto remains: *"Next!"* Forget about it, move quickly on to the next deal, and let the law of averages work its wonders.

Working long, hard hours. As to the myth about working long, hard hours, I came to the conclusion that the words *long* and *hard* are relative. What one person considers to be hard, someone else might think is coasting. What one person considers to be long hours may, by someone else's standards, be just getting by. The whole concept of hard work, then, tends to be subjective. It wasn't so much that I scorned hard work; I didn't—and still don't. I simply recognized that I should not allow myself to be intimidated by those who overemphasized the importance of "hard work." Subsequent observations through the years have, in fact, convinced me that I work harder and longer hours than most people who drone on endlessly about their labors.

Since "working long, hard hours" is a relative phrase, it logically follows that there is no set number of hours per day that one has to work in order to succeed. The amount of time you need to work each day depends upon your individual ability and the size of your goals. For example, a person of greater ability who desires to earn $100,000 a year might be able to accomplish that by working four hours a day, while someone of lesser ability who wants to earn $50,000 a year might find it necessary to work ten hours a day to accomplish his goals.

Also, there is a point of diminishing returns when it comes to putting in long hours. When energy is continuously expended over a long period of time, both the body and brain decrease their output, quantitatively and qualitatively. Naturally, everyone's body and brain have different tolerances, but nonetheless there is a point at which results begin to diminish in relation to the effort expended.

In fact, there's a point at which one's results actually become negative. It's an old axiom in football that a tired player is a player in danger of being injured. Likewise, a person who works too long at one stretch is in danger of making costly mistakes. Mental and physical fatigue are natural enemies of anyone who aspires to great success.

My answer to the "working long, hard hours" adage became known as the Uncle George Theory, which states: *If your main focus is on keeping your nose to the grindstone and working long, hard hours, you're guaranteed to get only one thing in return: old!*

One need only look at the empirical evidence to confirm the soundness of this theory. Have you not seen, with your own eyes, that working long, hard hours does not by itself assure a person of success? In this regard, I often think of my Uncle George, who served as my inspiration for the Uncle George Theory. This kindly little gentleman owned a corner grocery store and worked fourteen- to sixteen-hour days all his life. He never succeeded in getting rich, but he did get old. This didn't take any great amount of insight on my part, just good eyesight. I could see, with my own eyes, the hours and effort my uncle put into his work every day, and I could also see that it never got him anywhere.

Everyone has an Uncle George. Of course, your Uncle George might be a cousin, a brother, or perhaps your own father—someone who has worked very hard over the years, kept his nose to the grindstone, yet never achieved any great degree of success. Whenever you've witnessed such a sad drama playing out, you were observing, firsthand, the inherent truth in the Uncle George Theory.

Perhaps you're thinking that the world is unjust, and no doubt you're right. All I know is that I didn't lay down the framework of reality; I just learned to acknowledge it. The reality of the Uncle George Theory is self-evident to anyone who has a serious desire to discover truth. All that is required to accurately observe this fact of life is intellectual honesty. By acknowledging this truth, I was able to make it work *for* me rather than allowing myself to be intimidated by others into believing that hard work alone would make me successful.

The same goes here for what I said about having a positive mental attitude, i.e., that hard work does not *prevent* a person from being successful; on the contrary, as previously stated, a good work ethic is crucial to success. The point of the Uncle George Theory is that hard work alone does not *assure* anyone of success. I never had a problem with working long, hard hours, but I didn't start making any serious money until I supplemented my hard work with the philosophy I set forth in this book.

By gaining an understanding of what a positive mental attitude means in real-life terms, and by realizing that working long, hard hours doesn't guarantee success, my mind became a clean slate that was open to new ideas—ideas based on reality rather than myths. And in order to construct a workable success philosophy, one that would be able to stand up to the punishment of real-world experiences, I knew I would have to build a strong foundation to replace the old one that had not worked in actual practice.

To accomplish this, I undertook an in-depth study of my own past experiences. I tried to be painfully honest in identifying the factors that had contributed to my failures, as well as those that had led to success. I then began piecing together an overall philosophy based on my conclusions. Though there have been no fundamental changes in my philosophy through the years, the natural process of maturation assures that I will continually find the need to fine tune it. I never cease to be amazed at how each new experience teaches me a new, often subtle, twist that I hadn't thought of before. It continually reminds me how exciting it is to grow and evolve intellectually to the very end of one's journey through life.

CHAPTER 2

REPLACING THE MYTHS

Four of the theories discussed in this chapter represent the cornerstones of my reality-based philosophy and are anchored to a fifth theory that I look upon as the bedrock of my philosophy. I use the word *bedrock* because without it I surely would have spent the rest of my life as an intimidatee.

The bedrock theory I am referring to is the Theory of Reality, which states: *Reality is neither the way you wish things to be nor the way they appear to be, but the way they actually are. Either you acknowledge reality and use it to your benefit, or it will automatically work against you.*

This sounds so elementary at first blush that you might question why it would deserve the exalted status of being the bedrock my entire philosophy. Yet, no matter how simplistic it

16

may sound, it has been my observation that while most people pay lip service to the importance of correctly perceiving reality, very few of them demonstrate, through their actions, that they're really serious about welcoming reality into their daily lives. Which is unfortunate, because, in my opinion, the single biggest cause of failure lies in the inability to recognize and/or refusal to acknowledge reality.

Like a majority of people, I spent many years clinging to idealistic beliefs about how the world works. For years, I accepted traditional nostrums and confused the way I would have liked things to be with the way they really were. In retrospect, I am amazed at how I managed to limp along, year after year, refusing to acknowledge reality in the face of one ugly result after another.

I witnessed many people stubbornly adhering to conventional success rules, only to continually have their fingers severed when they reached for their chips. Their *wish* was that these rules would work; the *reality* was that they did not. I myself had a masochistic tendency to focus on the other person's best interest, particularly in business dealings, naively clinging to the belief that my benevolent attitude would be appreciated and that I would be handsomely rewarded. At best, I ended up with a handful of air; at worst, I got a financial slap in the face. My *wish* was that I would be justly rewarded for my goodwill attitude; the *reality* was that I was not.

Like millions of people before me, I went into one deal after another on just a handshake, believing the other party's assurances that a handshake was all that I needed—only to have him end up beating me over the head with his other hand! My *wish* was that I needed only a handshake; the *reality* was that I needed a clear, written agreement.

I repeatedly listened to attorneys insist that they weren't deal-killers—that they weren't like those "typical attorneys who concentrated on finding, rather than solving, problems" only to witness those same non-deal-killing attorneys blow one deal after another. My *wish* was that each new attorney proclaimed himself to be different from other (deal-killing) attorneys would show, through his actions, that he wasn't a deal-killer; the *reality*, however, was that the vast majority of such attorneys ended up being *worse* than most of their brethren.

I, like most people in the Business World Jungle, wished that the game of business took place on a nursery school playground; the reality, however, was that it was played in a vicious jungle. I concluded that I must either accept that reality or, for my own well-being, give up all my worldly possessions (a bicycle, clock radio, and tattered Mickey Mantle baseball card) and become a monk. I opted for the former.

In addition to people confusing their wishes with the way things really are, there's another important factor that can blind a person to reality: illusion. It's even more difficult and painful to recognize and deal with illusions than wishes, but one gut-wrenching experience after another forced me to became a hard-nosed realist. As a result, I ultimately made it a habit to relentlessly probe every deal for illusions, especially if a deal looked too good to be true.

THE FOUR CORNERSTONES

***Cornerstone No. 1* is the Theory of Relativity, which states:** *In order to settle on a rational course of action (or inaction), one must first weigh all pertinent facts in a relative light and carefully define his terms.*

Let's take honesty as an example. Everyone defines honesty to conveniently fit his own actions. Question: Have you ever met a person who admits to being dishonest? Second question: Have you ever *known* a dishonest person? I would probably be on pretty safe ground if I wagered that your answer to the first question was negative and your answer to the second question was affirmative.

Since I had dealt with many people whom I considered to be dishonest, yet had never known anyone who *admitted* to being dishonest, it was clear to me that a term like *honesty* was relative and subjective. In fact, every human being interprets everything in life to suit himself. I'm not just talking about *other* people; I'm talking about you and me as well. We can't help it; we're human. Unlike animals, human beings have the ability to intellectualize and interpret, so the key issue becomes objectivity versus subjectivity. Either through genetics or environment, or both, some human beings are better than others when it comes to being objective, and such individuals are much more likely to be rational in their interpretation of events. In any case, interpreting events with a bias toward our own well-being is a perfectly natural human trait.

Once I recognized that honesty was a relative and subjective characteristic, I realized that for years I had been operating under the delusion that there were only two types of people in the world: honest and dishonest. I now understood that a person could only be honest or dishonest relative to the facts in a given situation, or relative to some individual's personal moral standards. That being the case, if someone tells me that an individual I'm dealing with is dishonest, it's meaningless to me. I want him to carefully define what he means by *dishonest* in that particular instance so I can then decide if his definition is relevant to my objective.

As another example of relativity, I pointed out in Chapter 1 that what is hard work to one person might be semi-retirement to another. Hard work, in other words, is a relative notion. Are you working hard relative to how hard *you* usually work or relative to how hard *someone else* works? A phrase such as "working long, hard hours" has no meaning unless it is clearly defined by the user.

A final example of relativity is to be seen in the word *success*. There is no such thing as absolute success. You can only be successful relative to some standard, whether that standard be based on your own goals or someone else's achievements. When a person talks to me about success, I might have a completely different mental picture of success than he does. In order for us to have a rational discussion, he must first define what he means by *success*.

It's important not to allow yourself to be intimidated by relative or subjective words and statements that are meaningful only when examined in the clear light of relativity.

Cornerstone No. 2 is the Theory of Relevance, which states: *No matter how interesting or how true something may be, the primary factor to take into consideration is how relevant it is to your achieving main your objective.*

Early in my career, I tended to spend a great deal of time on projects that were, so to speak, side issues. As I became conscious of my error, I worked hard to develop the habit of qualifying every project by asking myself whether or not it would bring me closer to achieving my goals. If the answer was *no*, I eliminated it or put it on the back burner.

For example, once I understood the relevant factors in closing real estate sales, I noticed that a seller, in particular, had a tendency to dwell on facts about his property that were not relevant to its value. In particular, a seller invariably would talk a lot about how much it had cost him to build his apartment development, office building, or shopping center. But, while I may have had empathy for him, his cost of construction had no effect whatsoever on the prospective buyer's determination of the value of his property. If the seller had spent twice as much to build an apartment development as he should have, that was his problem, not the buyer's. The buyer of income-producing properties was primarily interested in cash flow, and had little, if any, interest in the seller's cost of construction.

Another example was when a seller would try to impress me with his honesty, and thus there was no reason to worry about my commission. Needless to say, a discussion of his honesty wasn't relevant. What *was* relevant, however, was whether or not he was willing to put into writing what we had agreed upon with regard to my commission. A discussion of honesty, then, is not only relative, but also *irrelevant* when it comes to business dealings. "Trust me" has become something of a cliché comedy line in the Business World Jungle.

Note that I did *not* say that honesty isn't relevant, but that a *discussion* of honesty is not relevant. In other words, parties to a transaction need not waste their time trying to impress each other with their honesty, as such time could be more efficiently employed working on a written agreement. In business, a written agreement is high on the list of relevant factors.

As a final illustration of the Theory of Relevance, whenever a seller wanted me to lower my commission (which was virtually 100 percent of the time) because he "hadn't realized how many additional expenses" he was going to have at the closing, that was not a relevant factor from my point of view. Sure, I may have been a good Samaritan and had empathy for the seller in such a situation, but that still didn't make his problem relevant to the commission we had agreed upon.

In fact, it was no more relevant than if I had proclaimed that I needed *more* money than our agreement called for, and that I would like my commission to be *increased.* How many sellers do you think would react favorably to *that* kind of logic? The only relevant factor was what our written agreement stated—period.

In becoming adept at recognizing what was and was not relevant, I found that it was not only important to try to keep buyers and sellers from drifting onto irrelevant tangents, but to keep my own attention focused on relevant factors. I became determined that I would not waste time and effort on issues that had little or nothing to do with my earning, and *receiving*, commissions.

Cornerstone No. 3 is the Mortality Theory, which states: *Given that your time on earth is limited, it makes good sense to aim high and move fast.*

When my participation in the game of life ends, I don't want to be caught begging for one more chance to grab the brass ring.

The fact is that I've never known a person who was given an extra inning. Most people block from their conscious minds the reality that they're going to die, and in a relatively short period of time, at that. I didn't like facing this reality any more than does anyone else, but I finally did so after the Theory of Reality became firmly entrenched in my thinking.

As a result, I quit hiding my head in the sand and faced the reality that I was as mortal as every person who has ever lived on this planet. I figured that, with some luck, I might be around for another fifty years or so. By the same token, circumstances beyond my control could reduce my secular visit to a matter of months, days, hours, or even minutes. There was simply no way of knowing.

If there is something beyond our worldly existence, what a great bonus that will be. However, I had no way of knowing for certain that there was anything beyond life on earth, so I decided to base my actions on the assumption that this time around would be my only shot. I made up my mind that I was not going to squander—because of fear, intimidation, or any other reason—what might be my only opportunity to win at the game of life. In the event I had only one life to live, I figured I had better get on with things as quickly as possible.

***Cornerstone No. 4* is the Ice-Ball Theory, which states:** *Given the apparent, ultimate fate of the earth, it is vain and nonsensical to take oneself too seriously.*

I call this the Ice-Ball Theory because of an ominous description of the earth's destiny that I read some years ago. The author explained that our sun is slowly burning out and that in 50 billion years or so it will be completely extinguished. When that occurs, the earth will be nothing but a frozen ball of ice. Accompanying the explanation was a chilling illustration of what the earth might look like at that time.

As ominous as the explanation and illustration were, I came to the conclusion that it was just another reality of life, that there was absolutely nothing I could do about it, and that, in light of this very long-term reality, the immediate problems plaguing me—particularly in the Business World Jungle—were so insignificant as to make me feel like an ant. The reality from my vantage point was that 50 billion years from now, when the earth is nothing but an ice ball, my problems of today will be too insignificant to have been recorded. Indeed, there would undoubtedly not even be a record of the entire century in which I had lived most of my life.

The Ice-Ball Theory is the flip side of the Mortality Theory coin. While on the one hand it's intuitive to make the most of the time you have left on earth, the Ice-Ball Theory eliminates stress and makes it possible for you to enjoy your quest for success. In fact, as most successful people have discovered, it's the striving and struggling for success, rather than success itself, that bring about the greatest amount of joy.

Having this kind of mind-set puts you at a decided advantage over competitors in your field who tend to view every deal as life or death. Stressed-out individuals tend to press too hard for results at crucial moments, and the harder someone presses for a result, the less likely it is he will achieve it.

Not taking myself too seriously helped me to look at life as a game, and at business as a sort of poker game within the bigger game of life. I pictured the earth as a giant poker table upon which the game of business is played, with only a fixed number of chips on the table. Each player gets to participate for an unknown period of time, and the name of the game is to see how many chips he can pile onto his stack.

(I should point out that years later, when I became a student of Austrian economics, I came to understand that, technically speaking, the number of "chips" is not fixed; quite the contrary, in fact. That's because more wealth is constantly being created, so business is not a zero-sum game. The stories in this book, however, relate to specific real estate deals, and rest assured that every real estate closing *is* a zero-sum game. That's because the buyer is only willing to come up with "X" amount of money, the seller insists on receiving "Y" amount of money, and if it turns out that "Y" just happens to equal "X"—which, for some mysterious reason, is usually the case—the real estate agent ends up with "Z" [as in *zero*] amount of money.] *That* is reality.

Of course, the chips themselves are of no particular use to anyone. In fact, financial gluttons have found, to their dismay, that either bathing in money or eating it are unsanitary habits that can cause one to become quite ill. However, chips do serve as a means to an end. The rules of the bigger game of life provide for the exchange of Jungle chips for material items that can improve the quality of a person's life.

You might be inclined to ask, "If life is nothing more than a game, why play so hard to win?" To which I would answer, Why *not* try to win—and, as a bonus, have some fun along the way? Maybe it's just me, but it seems like common sense. I therefore made the decision to go for all I could get, as quickly as I could get it, while I was still vital enough to play the game.

Recognizing that both life and business are games also made it easier for me not to take myself too seriously, which in turn made it that much easier to succeed. After all, if life is just a game, why be afraid to take chances? The reality is that there's no way that you're going to get out of the game alive anyway, so what's the point of being timid?

In the next chapter, I relate some tales of woe that I experienced prior to grasping the significance of the Ice-Ball Theory, and explain how these agonizing experiences helped me to further formulate my philosophy. As a result, I developed techniques not only to dramatically increase my earnings, but, more important, to make certain that I actually *received* what I earned.

And, of course, had it not been for my early understanding of the Theory of Next, I would never have been able to survive the seemingly endless number of heartaches, humiliations, and frustrations that I endured during those early years of trial by fire.

CHAPTER 3

PASSING MY ENTRANCE EXAM
AT SCREW U.

When I entered the real estate business, I was both ignorant and naïve, with absolutely no idea of the painful realities that awaited me. Little did I know that I
would be able to survive only because of two theories I had developed years earlier. Had it not been for these theories, I probably
would not have had the courage to become a real estate agent,
because the discouraging remarks that were gleefully directed at
me by many real estate brokers and salesmen would surely have
crushed my spirit.

It seemed that whenever I talked to people in the business
about what was involved in obtaining a real estate license, they
would go to great lengths to tell me how tough their profession
was, how it was almost impossible for a newcomer to get started,

how exceptional a person had to be to succeed as a real estate agent, and, in summation, why it would be a mistake for me to enter their field.

Years earlier, this kind of talk would have totally intimidated me, and I undoubtedly would have become convinced that I would be wasting my time to even make the effort. Fortunately, however, I had paid a lot of dues long before I decided to go into the real estate business, so I was able to ignore most of the negative grenades tossed at me. I had long before concluded that all members of the Discouragement Fraternity had two things in common: (1) Because they were insecure, they feared competition, and (2) they were ferocious about protecting their turf.

The two theories that helped me survive my entrance exam (i.e., hazing by the Discouragement Fraternity) at Screw U. (my early years in the real estate business) are the focus of this chapter.

The first one is the Tortoise and Hare Theory, which states: *The outcome of most situations in life are determined over the long term. The guy who gets off to a fast start merely wins a battle; the individual who's ahead at the end of the race wins the war. Battles are for ego-trippers, wars are for money-grippers.*

The Tortoise is the unglamorous plodder who always seems to find a way to come out ahead, though he has a habit of getting bruised and battered along the way. He isn't flashy or impressive. His strengths are consistency, perseverance, and resiliency.

The Tortoise is the quintessential antihero. Ben Braddock (played by Dustin Hoffman), the shy, stuttering boyfriend in *The Graduate,* was a classic antihero. He lost every battle, but somehow managed to win the war (the spoils of which were none other than Katharine Ross). Colombo, the fumbling, stumbling detective played by Peter Falk in the old TV series of the same name, was slow when it came to figuring things out, but in the end he always got his man. And how about Rocky Balboa (Sylvester Stallone) in the *Rocky* series? Tortoises all.

While still in my teens, I became conscious of the fact that I was a slow starter at most things, yet almost always seemed to find a way to finish strong. I finally concluded that it was my perfectionism that was at the heart of my slow starts. I had an inherent urge to have all the ground rules defined, study the lay of the land, prepare a game plan, and organize all the details before moving forward. I tried to (and still do) live by the words of Abraham Lincoln: "If I had eight hours to chop down a tree, I'd spend six sharpening my axe."

As a result of my methodical approach to projects, I began, in a tongue-in-cheek manner, to compare myself to the fabled tortoise in the tortoise and hare tale. I learned, over a period of time, that it was not so important to be the life of the party or the center of attention in a crowd. The important thing was what happened after the crowd dispersed. The big points are scored when you go one-on-one with someone behind closed doors.

More often than not, glibness in a crowd is just part of the "all show, no dough" syndrome. So, though I realized I was not particularly impressive on first meeting—especially in situations where three or more people were present—I found that I could be very effective by doggedly following up with one-on-one meetings at a later time.

I can't deny that it would be nice to have the kind of personality that would dazzle people on first encounter, and I wouldn't mind being a little faster out of the starting gate, either. The reality, however, is that I don't have these qualities, and even back in my teen-dumb days I recognized my shortcomings in these areas. And that, in turn, caused me to focus on playing the hand I had been dealt to the best of my ability.

Having christened myself "The Tortoise," my motto became: *If you slow down enough to look over your right shoulder, I'll pass you on the left; if you slow down enough to look over your left shoulder, I'll pass you on the right; and if you try to stop me from passing you on either side, I'll maneuver between your legs, if that's what it takes. That heavy breathing you hear behind you is me—steadily closing in on you.*

Or, in more direct terms: *Quickly getting out of the starting blocks may get people's attention, but all that counts is where you are when the race is over.*

In other words, a tortoise focuses on long-term results. If a stuttering shrimp like Dustin Hoffman could win Katharine Ross, who knows what treasures might lie ahead for a relentless, resourceful reptile? So, after years of playing the role of The Tortoise—of finding a way to win so many seemingly lost races—I was not going to allow myself to be intimidated by the Discouragement Fraternity when I entered the real estate business.

The second theory that played a major role in protecting me from the Discouragement Fraternity when I first entered Screw U. was the Organic Chemistry Theory, which states: *Don't allow yourself to be intimidated by know-it-alls who thrive on bestowing their knowledge on insecure people. Mentally close your ears and put blinders on your eyes, and move relentlessly forward with the knowledge that what someone else knows is not relevant. In the final analysis, what is most relevant to your success is what you know and what you do.*

This theory was derived from an experience I had at age twenty that forever changed my life. When I was in college, I took a curriculum that was required for application to—of all things—dental school. One of the required courses was organic chemistry, which also was one of the most dreaded of all undergraduate subjects. The course was so difficult that it had a 50-percent student failure rate.

After attending the first lecture, I became convinced that I, too, was destined to join the legions of students who had flunked organic chemistry. I had absolutely no idea what the instructor was talking about. For all I knew, a molecule was a spare part in an automobile engine. The worst, however, was yet to come.

On the second day, we had our first laboratory session and it was like a psychedelic nightmare for me. All I could see was one big blur of test tubes, acid bottles, and white aprons. I considered it to be a giant step forward when I finally located my laboratory desk. As I sat on my stool, displaying what would years later come to be known as the Dan Quayle look, I kept thinking that a savior-instructor would appear at the front of the laboratory at any moment and explain what we should be doing. No such luck. What was especially disconcerting to me was that all the other students in the lab appeared to know exactly what they were doing. Could this really be the road leading to Katharine Ross?

Then, all at once, I saw him—tall, slender, and sporting a blond crew cut and look of self-assurance that suggested both boredom (with how easy it all was) and disdain (for thick-headed reptiles like me). As big as life, there he was—standing right at the end of my laboratory row—the guy who was to be the focal point of one of the most important revelations of my life, a revelation that I would ultimately transform into a theory to help me snatch victory from the jaws of defeat time and time again, long after my graduation from Screw U.

Who was this tall, light stranger? None other than—Sound the trumpets!—a Court Holder. (In the coming years, I would find that Court Holders come in all shapes, sizes, and colors; i.e., tall and blond are by no means standard physical characteristics of this fascinating species.)

What qualifies an individual to be a Court Holder? It's really quite simple: A Court Holder is a person who makes a career out of holding court. He was the fellow at the last cocktail party you attended—the one standing poised and charming, one elbow on the mantle, a drink in his hand, and a group of information-starved puppies flocking around him in a semicircle—explaining how utterly simple it all is. Most important, a Court Holder is a master intimidator.

A truly professional Court Holder is not particular about where he holds court, either. He can do it just as effectively whether he's in a clubhouse locker room, at the office, or, by golly, in a chemistry lab. The only requirement for calling his court into session is that there be two or more information-starved, salivating puppies willing to listen to him pontificate. Of course, the more puppies the Court Holder has in his court, the better he likes it. And the more wide-eyed they are with awe, the more inspired he is to sprinkle smatterings of his seemingly infinite knowledge around the court.

My eyes nearly bulged out of my head as I watched the Court Holder flipping test tubes around like a professional juggler, nonchalantly lighting his Bunsen burner backhanded and leafing through his laboratory workbook so quickly that I was certain he would finish the entire course in less than two days.

A crowd was quickly gathering around him. Hope shot into my heart as I bounded down the aisle toward this dazzling paragon of knowledge. Surely there must be a crumb or two of wisdom he could spare a hopelessly lost reptile like me. Surely he would not turn me away without his tip of the day.

I was in luck. As the Court Holder breezed through the laboratory experiments for that particular day, he graciously and simultaneously held court for a dozen or so puppies and one tortoise. He even took the trouble to answer a couple of my intellectually loaded questions, such as, "Er ... where do I obtain a key to my locker?" and "Who do I see about getting a laboratory apron?" without so much as looking up from his test tubes. I wasn't even granted a look of disdain like most of the other puppies in his court. I guess I was such a hopeless pudding head that I was considered to be an untouchable in organic chemistry circles. Nevertheless, for me it was true love. Fantasies of someday getting an autographed picture of this modern-day Einstein flooded my mind.

This pattern repeated itself for several weeks, though I eventually did succeed in getting both a laboratory apron and a key to my locker. However, I accepted the fact that I would never be anything but a lowly serf in the Court Holder's organic chemistry kingdom. That being the case, I decided to play the hand I had been dealt as best I could. I trudged ahead, tortoise style, studying my textbook hour upon hour each night. Yet, no matter

*"Oh, Great Blond One, where might I obtain
a key to my laboratory locker?"*

how much I studied, I never seemed to be quite up on what was being discussed in class, and I continued to be completely lost in laboratory. Regardless of how much time and effort I put into it, it was obvious to me that I would always be an untouchable in the eyes of his majesty, the Court Holder.

Then, one day, a funny thing happened on the way to court: We had an examination. As the instructor passed out the test, you could hear moans throughout the room as the students began to glance at the complex questions. Much to my surprise, however, whatever had been going on in laboratory during the preceding weeks evidently had been explained in the textbook (which I had virtually memorized), because the material on the test seemed pretty familiar to me.

When the exam was over, students came stumbling out of the classroom looking shell-shocked and talking in a thoroughly defeated manner. I was too embarrassed even to mention it, but, frankly, the questions had not seemed that difficult to me. Surely, I reasoned, I must have completely misunderstood the subject matter during my long and gut-wrenching study sessions. Why else would the test not have seemed very difficult?

When it came time for the test papers to be handed back to the class about a week later, fear filled the auditorium-size classroom. The instructor announced the grading curve (i.e., the grading scale based on averages) for the test as follows:

48 & up	A (excellent)
40–47	B (good)
26–39	C (average)
20–25	D (poor)
19 & under	F (give up and get a Burger King application)

The instructor told the class that the scores had ranged from zero to 105. (There had been two bonus questions, so it was theoretically possible to score 108 on the test.) He went on to say that, out of a class of approximately 300 students, the next highest grade (after the score of 105) was 58. The class gasped in unison. It was inconceivable that the second highest score in a class of 300 students was forty-seven points *lower* than the top grade.

The instructor said that it was only appropriate to hand out the paper with the near-perfect score of 105 first, and that he would then call the rest of the students in alphabetical order to come forward and get their results. The students sitting around the Court Holder began patting him on the back and elbowing him ("You sonofagun, you ..."), but he looked so bored by the certainty of it all that I thought he was going to fall asleep.

P.S. He should have. Impossible as it seemed, the Court Holder *didn't* get the 105. In fact, he didn't even get the 58. What this master intimidator did get was a solid 33, which placed him smack dab in the middle of the class. Inconceivable as it may have been, the reality was that the Court Holder was only average. He was, in fact, the Organic Emperor who had no clothes.

Of course, you've already guessed the punch line. You can imagine how embarrassed I was as I walked to the front of the room to pick up my 105 test score. Though I looked straight ahead during the remainder of the day's session, I could feel 300 pairs of eyes staring at me. Telepathically, I could hear the Court Holder's groupies wondering, "Who is this green, scaly character, anyway? I've never even noticed him in here before."

When the bell rang, I hustled out the door, feeling too self-conscious to talk to anyone. I immediately resigned from the court and breezed through the remainder of the course with a high "A." The only thing that put a damper on the remainder of the year for me was the uneasy feeling that the Court Holder was continually staring at me out of the corner of his eye during laboratory sessions. Egad, I loved his crew cut. Why in the heck did my hair have to be so fine that I couldn't get it to stand up straight even with gum tar? Ah, well, we can't have it all, can we?

Blessed Court Holder, wherever you may now be, I want you to know that I shall forever be indebted to you. Since my encounter with you in organic chemistry lab, I've met many members of your species, and in each case, because of my experience with you, I was able to quickly identify them as Court Holders. Further, I've had the self-confidence to ignore their intimidating ways and go for life's big payoffs without a shred of embarrassment. No doubt about it, it was that Hall of Fame Court Holder in organic chemistry who provided the first step toward my understanding that the refusal to be intimidated was a crucial element in winning.

In summation, if someone feels the psychological need to hold court, that's *his* business. Your job is to mind *your* business. Don't allow yourself to be intimidated by someone else's knowledge—or apparent knowledge. What another person knows or doesn't know will not affect *your* success one way or another, so from your standpoint it's an irrelevancy.

Armed with the Tortoise and Hare Theory and Organic Chemistry Theory, I now felt qualified and ready to enter that most revered of all institutions of higher learning, Screw U. These theories gave me the strength to withstand the negative barrages of intimidation directed at me by the Discouragement Fraternity, and the courage to forge ahead into the real estate business.

CHAPTER 4

MY THREE
UNFORGETTABLE PROFESSORS
AT SCREW U.

I refer to my first three years in the real estate business as my undergraduate days at Screw U. because it was during this time that I was forced, through firsthand experience, to come to grips with the realities of the Business World Jungle. In curriculum terms, you might say that my major was Reality and my minor was Real Estate.

Without question, the most important reality I discovered during those early years at Screw U. was that there are basically only three types of people in the business world. (There is actually a fourth type—the individual who stands to benefit directly as a result of your financial success; i.e., the more you make, the more he makes. However, the latter type, in its pure form, is a rare exception, so it need not be addressed in this book. My focus here is on those who do *not* stand to benefit from your success.)

Let's assume, for the moment, that you're a real estate agent and that you represent the owner of a property. It's nice to say that the owner will benefit by your success in selling his property, but, as discussed earlier, success is a relative word. Granted, he will benefit to the extent he receives money from the buyer, but he will not benefit by *your* success in collecting a real estate commission. Like it or not, it's a zero-sum game, so collecting your commission should be *your* main criterion for success. Selling the owner's property (which is *his* chief criterion for success) is but a means to *your* end.

The painful reality is that the less the real estate agent makes, the better it is for the seller (and, theoretically, the buyer, since the buyer is the one who comes up with the money that ultimately pays the real estate commission). And never forget that buyers and sellers understand all too well the Mideast proverb "the enemy of my enemy is my friend." If you have a commission or fee owing to you—*regardless* of the business you're in—*you* are the enemy of *both* principals! If you refuse to believe this fact of life, I suggest your save yourself years of grief and get a government job.

There's an old business adage that "the only way a deal works out is if everybody benefits from the transaction," and, in theory, it's true. But in real life, this philosophy doesn't seem to include deal "pests" who are owed fees and/or commissions for their work. In the real estate business, for example, the empirical evidence suggests that the word *everybody* refers only to the buyer and seller.

Regardless of the type of business you're in, the above example should help you understand why certain people may have been less than honest with you in past dealings. It may have been in their best interest to see you succeed, but their definition of success may not have included paying you what you earned. It's nice to get patted on the back and told what a dandy job you did, but that shouldn't be *your* definition of success. What you want is cash, not kudos.

What I'm talking about here is the Three-Type Theory, which states: *There are only three types of people in the business world (with the one exception noted above), as follows:*

Type Number One, *who lets you know from the outset—either through his words, his actions, or both—that he's out to get your chips. He then follows through by attempting to do just that.*

Type Number Two, *who goes to great lengths to assure you that he would never dream of pilfering your chips, often trying to throw you off guard by assuring you that he really wants to see you "get everything that's coming to you." Then, like Type Number One—and without hesitation—he goes about trying to grab your chips anyway.*

Type Number Three, *who, like Type Number Two, assures you that he's not interested in your chips. Unlike Type Number Two, however, he sincerely means what he says. But that's where the difference ends. Due to any one of a number of reasons—ranging from his own bungling to his amoral standards for rationalizing what's right and wrong—he, like Types Number One and Two, still ends up trying to grab your chips. Which means that his supposed good intentions are irrelevant to the final outcome.*

In summation, no matter how someone posits himself, you would be wise to assume that he will, in the final analysis, attempt to grab your chips.

So, even though someone may say that he wants to see you "get what's coming to you," that doesn't mean you have to believe it. Instead, you would be wise to count on human nature guiding the other person's actions when the money's on the table, and in turn rely on your own survival instincts to guard against an attempt to heist your chips.

Let me emphasize that if I could recreate the world so the above realities did not exist, I most definitely would. Alas, however, humility forces me to admit that I cannot alter human nature one iota. I am but a messenger, and, as such, am merely passing along to you what my *firsthand experience* at Screw U. taught me. Like it or not—and most people don't—the Three-Type Theory is simply a reality of Planet Earth.

In the next three chapters, I discuss (in the order in which they came into my life) three of my most exemplary professors during my undergraduate days at Screw U. These noble gentlemen will forever serve as my stereotypes for the three kinds of creatures who inhabit the Business World Jungle. They were high-level financial proctologists who did a marvelous job of teaching me how to identify other members of their species. The lessons I learned from them helped prepare me for their ruthless relatives who were lying in wait for me in the Jungle, and I shall forever be in their debt for sharing their wisdom with me.

CHAPTER 5

TYPE NUMBER THREE IS SINCERELY SORRY THAT HE GRABBED YOUR CHIPS, BUT THE RESULT IS JUST THE SAME AS IF HE WERE GLAD

What makes a Type Number Three so deadly is that he's neither menacing like a Type Number One nor diabolical like a Type Number Two. On the contrary, he has good intentions. He sincerely wants you to get a fair shake, but, due to some "unforeseen" circumstance(s), he somehow always seems to find himself in a position where he has "no choice" but to grab your chips.

The fact that he is genuinely sorry for having to screw you makes it difficult for you to show anger toward him. After all, the devil made him do it. In essence, what a Type Number Three is really saying to you when he separates you from your chips is: *"I really didn't mean to cut off your fingers, but I had no choice when you reached for your chips."*

My maiden contact with a Type Number Three came on my very first day at Screw U. I knew virtually nothing about real estate, let alone the warped psyches of buyers and sellers. Yet, as fate would have it, the first deal I worked on—a $5 million apartment complex in Cincinnati—was quite large for a newcomer to the business.

I had heard rumors that the two owners of the Cincinnati project, which was still partly under construction, were in serious financial trouble, so I decided to try a unique approach. I contacted one of the partners and, instead of inquiring about the possibility of listing his property for sale, asked him for a job. The way I phrased it was that I would like to "work on solving the financial problems (his) apartment development was experiencing." He told me that he couldn't afford to hire anyone, and, even if he could, he wouldn't hire me, because I had no previous real estate experience.

I quickly assured him that I could make up in energy, enthusiasm, and persistence what I lacked in knowledge and experience, but he continued to resist. Being the relentless tortoise I was, I finally offered to work for him on a "prove it or else" basis. I told him that I would work without a guaranteed salary and would even pay my own expenses, but if I solved the financial problems of his apartment development, I wanted to be "paid handsomely in return." Slave labor is always an appealing carrot to dangle in front of penny-pinching real estate developers, so, based on my everything-to-gain-and-nothing-to-lose proposition, he finally relented and allowed me to work on the project. Presto: On the strength of this shaky and vague verbal understanding, my real estate career was launched.

What I was counting on was the Law of Risk and Reward: *The less the risk, the lower the potential reward; the greater the risk, the higher the potential reward.* In a perfect world, a salesman would have no guarantees, but would also have no limit on what he could earn. If my first professor at Screw U. had agreed to put me on his payroll, it undoubtedly would have been at the legal minimum wage. As a result, I would have missed out on the opportunity not only to gain a great deal of knowledge about how the Business World Jungle works, but to earn some serious money right out of the starting gate. In fact, in retrospect—considering how valuable my experience with my professor turned out to be—I would have to say that, on a value-for-value basis, I probably should have paid *him* for all the knowledge and wisdom I acquired during the time I worked on his project.

The Cincinnati deal allowed me to learn early on that most of the cash-shortage problems real estate developers experience are a result of their undertaking projects without having much, if any, of their own cash invested in them. Nirvana for a real estate developer is to find a way to "finance out," i.e., to structure a project in such a way that he doesn't have to put any of his own money into it.

To accomplish this, most builders are masters at using mirrors, so to speak, to finesse their way from one project to another. An important talent in this regard is the art of ducking subcontractors who have the audacity to demand payment for their services, then ultimately paying off accrued construction debts through a pipe dream known as *cash flow.* (In most cases, the illusion of a positive cash flow is based on unrealistically low operating expenses and replacement costs. Down the road, of course, the Delusion Fiddler must be paid, and all too often payment comes in the form of a currency known as *bankruptcy.*)

My Type Number Three professor was pretty much of a silent partner in the Cincinnati project, and it was clear from the outset that he and the working partner ("Victor Vermin") were not on good terms (par for the course when financial problems set in). Victor lived in Cincinnati, and was on the building site every day overseeing construction. My Type Number Three professor's main contribution to the deal was that he had done the initial spade work in the planning and financing stages.

After a couple of weeks, I decided it was time to go to Cincinnati and speak directly with Victor, since I figured he would have a more up-to-date reading of the situation. Little did I know that it would turn out to be my Business World Jungle baptism. On several occasions, I set up appointments with Victor, traveled all the way to Cincinnati, then sat in his waiting room for as long as *eight hours*. Being the inexperienced twit that I was, I did not understand that Victor was a master intimidator, so I would just sit in his reception room and dutifully suck my thumb, play with my yo-yo, and read old issues of *Builder's Indigestion* twenty or thirty times.

One day, in particular, stands out in my mind. I had a firm appointment with Victor at 9:00 A.M., and, just to be on the safe side, I showed up at 8:45 A.M. Not only did Victor not acknowledge my presence all morning, but around noon he bolted out of his office with two other men and hurried right past me, without even a nod, on his way to lunch. Meekly, I called out to him and asked when he would be ready to meet with me. Without breaking stride, and barely looking back over his shoulder, he mumbled something that sounded like, "Back in a little while."

Why would I endure such humiliating treatment? Stupidity, to be sure. But, in fairness to reptiles throughout the world, it was the first real estate deal I had ever worked on. In addition, I was penniless (the world's most foolproof way to create humility), had no other deals in the hopper, and had no idea how to go about finding other deals.

So, at this early stage of my undergraduate studies at Screw U., it's not difficult to recall why, from my perspective, every deal was life or death. So much so that I felt I couldn't even take a chance on going out and grabbing a sandwich for lunch. After all, I didn't know when Victor might return to his office, and, after waiting all morning, I didn't want to take any chances on missing him when he returned.

When Victor finally showed up two hours later, I was a very hungry, very tired tortoise, so tired that I almost didn't look up in time to see him before he reached his office door. This time I called out in a much weaker, much more defeated voice, and

this time he totally ignored me. Unbeknownst to me at the time, what I was experiencing were the horrors a tortoise encounters when dealing from an inferior posture. As Victor's office door slammed shut, the thought of giving up entered my mind. Fortunately, however, the tortoise within me persisted, and I stubbornly sat in his reception room until 5:00 P.M. I finally got to talk with him only because, in desperation, I literally lunged in his path as he was leaving his office for the day.

After a series of punishing experiences like this, I finally learned that Victor had talked a mortgage banker into increasing the construction loan on his project and immediately advancing some additional funds, provided certain conditions were met. The most important of these conditions was that he was required to buy out my Type Number Three professor's interest in the development. I asked Victor how much he was willing to pay his partner, and, after thinking about it for a few minutes, he came up with a price, whereupon I told him that I would discuss his offer with my professor.

I then met with my professor and explained the situation, but packaged it a bit differently. The reason I did this was because not only was my agreement with my professor not in writing, even our verbal understanding did not spell out the precise amount of my fee. In fact, we had not even specified exactly what it was that I was supposed to accomplish in order to be entitled to my unspecified fee. All we had was a fuzzy understanding that I was supposed to be "paid handsomely" if I "solved the financial problems in Cincinnati." This is about as vague as an understanding can get in the Business World Jungle.

Closing a deal of one kind or another was beginning to look like a real possibility, and it was becoming obvious to me that I needed to get more specific with my professor. I reasoned that if I told him that Victor Vermin was prepared to pay the price that he (i.e., Victor) had just quoted me, and if that price was acceptable to my professor, neither of them would need me to make a deal. (In tortoise language, "Duhhh!") At a minimum, once my professor knew what Victor's offer was, he would be in a position to dictate to me what my reward should be.

I therefore told my professor only that I had been "kicking around some numbers with Victor," and, though I thought it would be a hard sell, there was a chance I might be able to get him to buy my professor's share of the project at a price that would get him (i.e., my professor) off the hook for most of the debts he had incurred in connection with the Cincinnati deal.

Then, I went a step further, because I was concerned that the price Victor had quoted me was so low that it might only succeed in angering my professor. Based on what he had told me about the extent of his financial problems, I was pretty certain that the suggested buy-out price would not completely bail him out of his financial difficulties. So I quoted him an even *lower* price than the one Victor had suggested, emphasizing that this was probably the best I could hope to do.

It was the age-old game of "I go low, you go high, and we compromise in the middle." (This simple strategy works just as well today as it did for merchants and traders in ancient China, Mesopotamia, and Greece. Why? Because human nature never changes. Only a fool—or an intelligent but naïve person—gives his best offer right off the bat.) Even though I had only recently enrolled at Screw U., I instinctively knew that my professor would want to negotiate the price upward no matter *what* the initial figure was that I quoted him. That being the case, my objective was to negotiate up *to* Victor's offering price rather than have to negotiate upward *from* that price. Never forget: Human beings are genetically programmed to *always* want more.

As I suspected would be the case, my professor's initial reaction was that the price I had suggested was absolutely unacceptable. However, after several days of discussions and many persistent and persuasive tortoise remarks later, I was able to get my professor to see that, in the long run, it would be better for him if I could "talk Victor into" buying him out at a price roughly equal to the one that (unbeknownst to my professor) Victor had *already* said he would be willing to pay.

I further convinced my professor that the project was destined to get into ever more financial trouble (which turned out to be a correct assessment on my part), and that he would be much better off to bail out now, get off the hook for any personal liability he had incurred, and still manage to come up with enough cash to pay off at least some of his other debts. In retrospect, considering all these factors, I probably did him a greater service than any other buyer or seller for whom I subsequently worked.

I should point out that in order to arrive at the price I quoted my professor, I *subtracted* $6,500 from the price Victor had told me he would be willing to pay. The $6,500 cushion represented the fee I arbitrarily decided would be a reasonable payment for my services for "solving the financial problems in Cincinnati." Feigning an afterthought, I then casually told my professor that I would try very hard to increase the price that he had tentatively agreed to (i.e., the amount that was $6,500 *lower* than Victor's offering price) by "five or ten thousand dollars" so I could "get a little something out of the deal, too." My professor nodded his head indifferently. After all, anything I got "over and above" what he was supposed to receive was of no interest to him, right?

Not exactly. The reality was that it was purely academic, as is always the case with fees and commissions, regardless of the kind of business you're in. It was, in fact, a simple matter of "psychological packaging." All I did was create the *illusion* that whatever fee I received would be over and above what my professor was willing to accept. The *reality* was that the less I received as a fee, the more money my professor would pocket. Anyone who aspires to success in any field of endeavor would do well to become adept at psychological packaging, or else be prepared to be victimized by a nasty little human trait called *greed*. This is *especially* true when dealing with supposedly "good guys" who seem genuinely sincere about wanting to see you get paid. Good intentions are swell and all that, but never bet against greed!

I now sensed that it was time to move in for the kill. I meekly asked my professor if he would mind signing "a simple little document" saying that the *net* price we had discussed was agreeable to him. I assured him that the only reason for wanting something in writing was to "have something in my hand" when I tried to "persuade" Victor to accept my professor's "offer" (which, I again emphasize, was $6,500 *lower* than the amount Victor had already agreed to pay).

You're probably wondering why I was dumb enough to show Victor a document that stated that my professor would take *less* than Victor had offered. Didn't I realize that Victor would simply lower his offer to match the figure my professor had agreed to? Of course I realized it! The answer is that I *didn't* show him the document. Show Victor Vermin the agreement that spelled out my commission? Are you kidding? Victor ate little kids for breakfast and didn't bother to spit out the bones. He rooted for the Atlantic Ocean in *Titanic*. Charles Manson was his idol. Victor was a classic, avaricious, mean-spirited real estate developer who took great delight in nickel and diming his adversaries to death—and anyone to whom he owed money was an adversary.

My real purpose for having my professor sign the "letter of understanding" was not just to "have something in my hand" when I went to Cincinnati, but to have something in writing regarding my fee. Once my professor had signed on the dotted line, I casually told him that I would probably use $6,500 as a "working number" for my fee, *tack it on* to the figure he and I had discussed, then put the total figure into the document as the price he had agreed to accept from Victor.

It was on-the-job training in psychology and phraseology. When you deal with sick minds, never waste time trying to become a healer. The most humane act you can perform for such a person is to state things in such a way that it will make him feel better about how things work out—*especially* if it involves your getting paid. After all, you can cause him a great deal of stress if you allow him to believe that he might actually be paying you what he owes you.

To make it appear almost as an afterthought, I purposely put the sentence about my $6,500 fee near the bottom of the document. In later years, I realized that my instincts, even at that early stage of my undergraduate days at Screw U., had been very good, because again and again I was to find that "afterthought" was a pretty accurate description of how most sellers view a real estate agent's commission. (Never state, in an agreement, what you want out of the deal *before* stating what the other party is going to get, because the other guy doesn't give a hoot about what *you* want. All he's interested in is what's in it for *him*. This is especially true of people who insist that "in order for a deal to work out, everyone has to be satisfied." Forget such babble; it's a fairy tale that will only cause you to drop your guard and lose some fingers in the process.)

Subsequent to my professor's signing the document, I again went back to Victor and emphasized what a hard sell it had been for me to get his partner to agree to his buy-out figure, but that I finally succeeded. Just as I had packaged my presentation of the deal in such a way that my professor would think of my fee as "over and above" what he was getting out of the deal, I also had to be certain that Victor didn't get any cute ideas about being able to save $6,500 by merely changing his original buy-out price to one that was equal to the net figure my professor had agreed to accept. As far as Victor knew, the original price he had discussed with me (again, an amount equal to the price my professor had agreed to *plus* my $6,500 fee) was the one my professor was willing to accept.

I told Victor that my professor was very uneasy about the deal, and that I could not guarantee that he wouldn't change his mind if we didn't proceed promptly. This got his attention. Feeling that it might be his only opportunity to get his partner out of the deal at a price he considered to be a bargain, Victor did everything he could to help bring about a quick closing.

Of course, with my professor I played it 180 degrees opposite, emphasizing how difficult it had been for me to get Victor to agree to "his" figure (the one that *included* my $6,500 fee). Just as I had done with Victor, I emphasized that I didn't know how long I could keep Victor committed to the deal, and urged him to do everything possible to help get it closed.

As closings go, this was as good as it gets, because all three parties involved—the buyer, the seller, and the real estate agent— were working hard to accomplish the same objective. Then, as we progressed toward a closing, I observed a phenomenon I was later to discover occurs prior to most real estate closings. My professor "sharpened his pencil" (his words) and continued to find one cost after another that he either had not previously considered or hadn't known about. How convenient. (In later years, this kind of talk got so old that I had to restrain myself from yawning.)

My professor was a classic Type Number Three. Virtually everyone who had ever dealt with him thought he was a nice guy and "basically" honest, but that he had experienced a string of bad luck that had caused him to "unintentionally" damage a lot of people along the way.

The closer we got to the closing, the more my professor sharpened his pencil. Being a Type Number Three, he was very nice about it and never came right out and said that he did not intend to pay my fee. He just mumbled a lot of negatives, and the more figuring he did, the more he mumbled—and the more concerned I became.

In fact, my concern became so great that I dared to ask myself a question that only an inexperienced reptile like me would dare ask: "If the buyer and seller in a real estate deal are represented by attorneys at a closing, why shouldn't the real estate agent also be represented by an attorney?" Sort of like the first ape in the *Planet of the Apes* movie who had the audacity to say, "No!" to a human being's command.

After all, didn't I have a vested interest in the deal, too? Nonetheless, every time the question crossed my mind, I thought to myself that if I showed up at the closing with an attorney, my professor would take it as an insult to his integrity and probably use it as an excuse not to pay me anything at all. In a sense, I was being intimidated by my own thoughts.

Finally, the big day arrived—my first real estate closing. I talked to my professor just a couple of hours before the closing was scheduled to take place, and, in typical Type Number Three fashion, he expressed sincere concern for my position. He said he felt terrible about it, but, after adding up all the figures, there was no way he could spare even $100 out of the proceeds of the closing, let alone $6,500.

I found his remark to be quite fascinating. I wondered how he could talk in terms of not being able to "spare" when it wasn't even his money he was talking about. Those were *my* chips he was referring to. They weren't his to spare! In addition, I thought to myself that whether or not my professor "felt terrible about it" was irrelevant. "Forget the niceties," I thought to myself, "and just fork over my chips."

My professor then assured me that in the "not too distant future" he would "see to it" that I would get "every dime that was coming to (me)." Sure, prof, no problem. He said he was working on a number of deals (all pie-in-the-sky, I might add), and that some were certain to close soon, at which time he would have plenty of cash with which to pay me. Sure, prof. In other words, he was telling me, "I'm sticking it to you now, but trust me not to do it to you down the road." I figured the next thing he would do is pull out a picture of Ebbets Field and say, "By the way, I have a nice property in New York that you might be interested in selling."

Luckily for me, I was stone broke. If I had been in a financial position to wait a few months, or even a few weeks, I probably would have backed off, given that I was still at a very easy to intimidate stage of my development. But I was so pushed to the wall that I could not wait even one more day, let alone weeks or months.

But I didn't say anything menacing to my professor, because I didn't want to put him on guard. Instead, in response to the "concern" he expressed for me, I just mumbled that I would see him at the closing and that "perhaps there might be a way to work something out." He gave me a "Sure, no problem" nod that I later realized was used in the Jungle as a euphemism for "Yeh, sure, anything you say; just take a hike."

I then made a bold decision. I scurried over to the office of an attorney friend of mine, showed him the document my professor had signed, described the conversation I had just had with him, and explained that the closing was about to take place. The attorney and I then went over to my professor's office and found that all the parties involved were in the process of preparing for the closing.

Whereupon my attorney sat down with the other two lawyers, and the *three* of them went through the mechanics of finalizing the deal. Although I didn't understand the principle at the time, what I had going for me at that closing was the unwritten, universally accepted understanding among all attorneys that I subsequently dubbed the Universal Attorney-to-Attorney Respect Rule. It's kind of analogous to "honor among thieves." In street parlance, the unwritten rule among lawyers is: You can rape and pillage civilians, but don't mess with the good fellas in the club. The simplest way to illustrate this law is to remind you of the last time you were a party to a lawsuit and how the attorneys for both sides left the courtroom, arm in arm, while discussing their upcoming Sunday golf game. Doesn't it warm the cockles of your heart to see the guy to whom you're paying $300 an hour shmoozing with the attorney who is trying to destroy you?

While the lawyers proceeded with the closing, I chatted with my professor and Victor Vermin about the weather, extraterrestrial life, and the merits of Metamucil. Sure, it was embarrassing, but I sucked it up inside and tried to convey a matter-of-fact attitude. I just kept asking myself, "Why *shouldn't* a real estate agent

"Did you guys happen to read the National Enquirer article about extraterrestrials preferring Metamucil in the travel-packet size?"

also be represented by an attorney at a closing?" After all, I was too inexperienced to know any better, right?

P.S. I got my $6,500 fee—*at the closing.*

Finally, in case you're wondering, I should point out that I have never doubted the propriety of my creative handling of this transaction, because I had thought it out carefully in advance and felt that my actions were justified on at least three counts:

First, not only did I not have a written agreement with my professor, I didn't even have a clear verbal agreement. Our understanding was vague, at best. All I had done was volunteer to try to "solve the financial problems in Cincinnati" and, if "successful" (which also was not defined), I was supposed to be "paid handsomely in return." In other words, there was no agreement, written or verbal, that morally obligated me to present my professor with offers to buy out his interest in the property. I was strictly on my own, and my fiduciary responsibility was to myself.

Second, as it turned out, everything I did was, in fact, in my professor's best interest. As I mentioned earlier, after analyzing the figures, I became convinced that the project was headed for even more financial difficulties, and my analysis turned out to be accurate. I also was convinced that I would never be able to work out a deal if I presented my professor with Victor Vermin's real offering price. By being a little creative, I did him a great service by helping him to avert what would have been a financial catastrophe for him later on. The bottom line is that both partners ended up being satisfied with the result, the proof being the fact that they agreed in writing to the final terms of the deal. It may not have been the deal either of them wanted, but it was a deal they were both willing to accept at that time and under the circumstances that then existed. It's called free-market capitalism.

Third, and most important from the standpoint of the theme of this book, is that the events at the closing proved that I had more than ample reason to be cautious about how I handled the negotiations. When it got down to the short strokes, my Type Number Three professor's actions left no doubt in my mind that

I would have walked away from the closing with nubs for fingers had I not taken precautions to protect my own interest as well as his.

How fortunate I had been. I had learned firsthand about the deadliness of Type Number Threes without having to experience the sick feeling that comes from having one's chips pilfered at the eleventh hour. Had my Cincinnati deal not ended on a happy note, it's very possible that I might not have been able to continue in the real estate business due to my precarious financial situation.

In addition to learning how a Type Number Three operates, I received a bonus in this deal in that I got an answer to my naive question, "Why shouldn't a real estate agent also be represented by an attorney at a closing?" Firsthand experience had emphatically given me the answer: "He should!"

Regardless of the business you're in, never allow yourself to be intimidated into believing that you aren't entitled to the same rights as the so-called principals in a deal. I say *so-called* because, from your standpoint, you *are* a principal. If you have a vested interest in a deal, you have a right to protect that interest, regardless of the size of your stake relative to the other players' shares. Just don't expect the other principals to agree with your viewpoint. To be forewarned is to be forearmed.

CHAPTER 6

TYPE NUMBER ONE ISN'T SORRY THAT HE GRABBED YOUR CHIPS, BECAUSE HE WARNED YOU AHEAD OF TIME HOW HE PLAYS THE GAME

Although I wasn't aware of it, I was already familiar with Type Number Ones prior to my entering Screw U. Because he wears a black hat, a Type Number One is quite easy to spot. He doesn't hide the fact that he's out to grab as many chips as possible and that anyone who attempts to grab any chips for himself is viewed as an adversary. In other words, he doesn't try to be clever; he lays his cards on the table from the outset. What a Type Number One is saying to you when he squeezes the last dollar from your deal is: *"I really meant to cut off your fingers, just as I told you I would, and before you reached for your chips you should have remembered my warning."*

In this respect, one might be justified in arguing that a Type Number One is the most honest of the three types of people in the Business World Jungle. Yet, prior to my experiences at Screw U., I thought the word *crook* was a pretty good description of a Type Number One. It wasn't until I became more educated that I was able to see that if a Type Number One's menacing gestures give you reason for concern, the solution is simple: Exercise your option of not becoming involved with him.

On the other hand, if you do decide to become involved in a business transaction with a Type Number One, there should be no doubt in your mind (assuming you're not sleepwalking) about his intentions. If you end up with a few less fingers, it's likely because you either refused to acknowledge the dangers of dealing with a Type Number One or you simply weren't prepared. You delude yourself if you try to claim that you were drawn into a transaction under the guise that you thought you would be dealing with someone who would be generous with you. Anyone who has spent more than a day at Screw U. knows a Type Number One on sight.

My Type Number One professor was an elderly gentleman who had accumulated considerable wealth through his vast knowledge of the real estate business, and he proved to be an excellent teacher. He had a dignified demeanor, but would not hesitate to cut out your heart if you failed to live up to your side of an agreement. At his age and financial station in life, he didn't need any more chips, so it was the pure fun—the thrill of crushing desperate real estate developers—that attracted him.

Like so many positive experiences in life, coming in contact with my Type Number One professor happened on a lark. After attending Screw U. for several months, I concluded that there was a big demand among real estate developers for secondary financing. Since most builders were desperate for money to keep their paper empires from collapsing, it seemed to me that this was an area of the real estate business where it would be easy to locate and sign up deals.

I happened to run across my professor's name while looking through a directory of capital sources in an effort to locate second-mortgage lenders. He specialized in making large second-mortgage loans on income-producing properties such as apartment developments, shopping centers, and office buildings.

My professor turned out to be a stern taskmaster who often tongue-lashed me for being too trusting. Whenever my inclination was to give a prospective borrower the benefit of the doubt, his position was that there was no such thing as "benefit of the doubt" in business dealings. His idea of an everyone-wins deal was to tie the other guy's hands behind his back, bind his feet, close off all avenues of escape, then "negotiate."

It was through my Type Number One professor that I first learned about one of the most important weapons that all wealthy people have at their disposal: *staying power*. I marveled at how he was prepared to walk away from any deal, because there was no one deal that was that important to him. As a result, he could not be intimidated.

The first deal he and I worked on together clearly demonstrated his hard-ball approach. I had brought him a $150,000 second-mortgage loan application from a desperate builder who was willing to put up nine small apartment properties as collateral. My professor expressed an immediate interest in the loan, and when I relayed that fact to the prospective borrower, he became very anxious to have him come to town and inspect his properties. The situation was ideal for my professor: The prospective borrower was anxious; my professor could care less. If you're on the anxious end of this kind of equation, you have two strikes against you before negotiations even begin.

After my professor inspected the prospective borrower's properties, he shook his head discouragingly and said that he would need more collateral in order to make the loan. The owner protested, insisting that the nine properties he was prepared to put up as security constituted more than sufficient collateral. My professor courteously thanked the builder for his time, then said that, under the circumstances, he would be leaving for the airport right away to try to catch an earlier flight back to New York. It was an eye-opening experience to witness a professional intimidator in action.

The prospective borrower, desperate for cash, looked like he was going to have apoplexy. He quickly backed off and agreed to give my professor, as additional collateral, a first mortgage on a 10-acre parcel of land that he said was in the process of being rezoned for industrial usage.

My professor not only accepted the land as additional collateral, but, as we got nearer the closing, insisted on inserting a clause in the loan agreement stipulating that if the land was not rezoned within 12 months, he could require the borrower to pay off an additional $20,000 on the principal of the loan. This struck me as a rather harsh condition, particularly since it appeared that the nine apartment properties alone were more than sufficient collateral for the second mortgage. But, as it turned out, I had only witnessed the tip of the iceberg. My professor's niftiest moves were yet to come.

Just as it began to appear that all the details for a closing had been worked out, and with the borrower looking ten years older than when the negotiations had begun, my professor— "after reviewing the figures very carefully"—said there was no way he could make a $150,000 loan based on the collateral they had been discussing. He told the borrower that due to this lack of collateral, $100,000 was the biggest loan he was willing to make.

At that point, the borrower became outwardly hostile. He adamantly refused to the lower loan figure, which prompted my professor to once again thank him for his time and indicate that he had better things to work on. Result? You guessed it—the borrower limped back to the "negotiating table." They finally "compromised" at $105,000—meaning that the borrower had to put up *more* collateral for *less* money! By this time the borrower was beyond desperate, and rest assured that his desperation did not go unnoticed by my professor. Before he was finished, my prof took advantage of his intimidating posture to land two final blows.

First, he required that the borrower deposit with him, each month, one-twelfth of the annual real estate taxes on each of the properties. This meant that the professor would have the use of the borrower's tax money until the real estate taxes were actually due, which in turn deprived the borrower of the use of his own funds.

The second blow, however, was the coup de grace. When my Type Number One professor examined the "rent rolls" for each of the properties, he noticed that one of the buildings, the construction of which had just been completed, still had a considerable number of vacancies. He insisted that $20,000 of the $105,000 loan be retained by him until that property reached an occupancy rate of approximately 80 percent. The same protests on the part of the borrower; the same threats of departure on the part of my professor; the same result: The borrower ended up agreeing to *all* of my professor's conditions.

Looking back on this deal, I now realize that it was actually just a matter of at what point the lender was willing to display mercy. He had the cash; the borrower was desperate. He had the staying power; the borrower was running out of time. He was intimidating; the borrower was intimidated. It was my Type Number One professor's favorite—and only—kind of deal: *totally one-sided.*

Again, in retrospect, I had the good fortune of earning while learning. I received a nominal loan-brokerage fee for my work, while having the honor of observing, at close range, how a high-level Type Number One plays the game. It was painful to witness—sort of like watching a lion devour a gazelle on one of those animal shows on TV—but very educational.

As the professor and I walked out of the building where the closing had taken place, I told him that the borrower seemed like a nice guy and that I hoped he would be able to abide by all the conditions of the loan agreement. To which my professor displayed his best Godfather-like smile and replied, "That's not possible." Puzzled, I asked him what he meant by that, whereupon he said,

"If you take the trouble to read the agreement carefully, you'll see that he was technically in default the moment he signed it."

Now *that's* what you call a practical course at Screw U!

In the months following the closing, the old man began to take a personal liking to me. I think he was impressed by my persistence and attention to detail, and, because of his own no-nonsense nature, my straightforward manner. I was neat and accurate in my presentations, and if additional information was needed to decide whether or not to proceed further with a deal, I obtained it immediately, even if it meant traveling a great distance at my own expense to secure the necessary details. Fortunately for me, I had been well aware of the importance of being willing to go the extra mile from having observed my father's work ethic from the time I was a small child.

Early on it appeared to me that my professor realized it was in his best interest to see me make money. He obviously reasoned that the more money I made, the more I would be encouraged to work hard to bring him as many prime deals as possible. So even though he was an orthodox Type Number One, he also qualified as one of those rare exceptions I spoke about earlier; i.e., with regard to his relationship with me, my getting paid actually benefited him in the long run.

Further, because it was also in *my* best interest to see *him* make money, I went out of my way to protect my professor in every deal. To many of our clients, I became cynically known as his watchdog. If there was one thing I recognized even then, it was on which side my bread was buttered. The old man and I had a wonderful relationship, because it was based on the most honest foundation that any business relationship can have: value for value.

As harsh as he was with me at times, I not only acquired a great deal of knowledge from my Type Number One professor, I actually grew fond of him. (I think it might have been his razor-sharp teeth that held me in awe.) Regardless of his take-no-prisoners philosophy, I respected him for his candor. I would hate to think how much longer it might have taken me to learn many crucial realities of the Business World Jungle had I not had the opportunity to work closely with my Type Number One professor for two solid years. He died a short time after I went on to graduate school, but, wherever he is today, I'd be surprised if he isn't still threatening desperate borrowers with wanting to go to the airport to catch an earlier flight home.

CHAPTER 7

TYPE NUMBER TWO ISN'T SORRY THAT HE GRABBED YOUR CHIPS, BECAUSE, IN SPITE OF HIS ASSURANCES TO THE CONTRARY, THAT WAS HIS INTENTION FROM THE OUTSET

Given that a Type Number One is easy to spot, there's no excuse for not learning how to defend yourself against him. And a Type Number Three, because of his sincerity and easygoing manner, can usually be made to behave by simply confronting him with the proper legal tools. But being trapped in a cage with a Type Number Two is not a good idea even for experienced, educated Jungle inhabitants. Until you learn the art of dealing with Type Number Twos, your progress in the Business World Jungle will be painstakingly slow—and unpleasant.

When a Type Number Two performs chip-replacement surgery on your wallet, all he's saying to you is: *I meant from the outset to cut off your fingers when you reached for your chips, even though I assured you that was not my intention.*

A Type Number Two is treacherous, not only because he's hard to recognize, but because he's a meat eater—in fact, the most vicious of all carnivores. To put it in perspective, think of it this way: A Type Number Two is to the Business World Jungle as Tyrannosaurus Rex is to Jurassic Park. Because he's cunning, a Type Number Two can sometimes be mistaken for either a Type Number One or Type Number Three. Deviousness is his stock in trade.

It was not until I had completed Anti-Deceit Measures 401 with my Type Number Two professor that I was prepared to graduate from Screw U. Not that I had never encountered a Type Number Two before. It's just that in the past I had failed to recognize members of this cannibal sect for what they really were, let alone study their sinister methods.

Like his fellow faculty members, Types Number One and Three, my Type Number Two professor at Screw U. was not only a perfect model of his species, but a great teacher as well. He was co-owner of an apartment-development company that had built a significant number of large apartment projects in the Midwest and on the East Coast. My initial contact with him came about as a result of making cold calls in an effort to solicit new second-mortgage deals. He expressed an immediate interest in meeting with me, and I made an appointment to come visit him.

When I went to his office for our first face-to-face discussion, I was impressed to the point of being awed. My Type Number Two professor spent an inordinate amount of time expounding on the virtues of dealing only with people who possessed buckets of integrity and the highest ethical standards—like himself, for example—*an almost sure sign that the person with whom you are speaking is a rapist, murderer, or, worst of all, an unethical real estate developer.* To boot, he casually tossed around the names of a sampling of competitors as examples of people whom he considered to be of questionable repute.

Talk about holier than thou, my new mentor was in a class by himself. And talk about gullible, The Tortoise ate up every

"Listen up, greenhorn, it's important to deal only with people of integrity—like me, for example."

word. I hadn't been so enamored since the first time I had laid eyes on the legendary Court Holder in organic chemistry lab years earlier. I once again found myself conjuring up fantasies of an autographed picture hanging over my hearth. I sat there listening to his fecal chatter as though I had just undergone a discount lobotomy, nodding my head up and down on cue to show that I was in total agreement with such clichés as, "Life is too short to deal with unethical people." I oohed and aahed as he name-dropped big institutions that had financed some of his projects or supposedly wanted to lend him money for future developments. He was wearing a white hat so tall that it nearly touched the ceiling, and his Che Guevara grin had the aura of a neon sign flashing the words, "Trust me."

When we finally got down to talking business, he told me that his company "could possibly use a couple million dollars to take advantage of some other opportunities." (Unbeknownst to me at the time, this was wheeler-dealer code for: "I'm in desperate financial straits and need a quick cash injection to avoid bankruptcy.")

He then mentioned that he owned a large apartment development in St. Louis, and that he might be interested in selling it outright rather than obtaining a second mortgage. He indicated, however, that it would take a purchase price in the area of $10 million for him to seriously consider selling. Here, too, I was too much of a neophyte to understand that no matter how convincing a prospective seller may appear to be about not being interested in selling his property for less than a certain price, he is almost always either lying or will eventually cave in and lower his price when a serious buyer enters the picture. Nothing changes a seller's view of the world quicker than a checkbook being waved in his face.

As my Type Number Two professor continued to pontificate, I did some rough figuring and concluded that if I was successful in selling his property, I could earn a commission in the area of $200,000–$300,000 based on the Board of Realtors' suggested commission scale. Such thinking only served again to demonstrate how much of a greenhorn I was at the time. Nothing worse than a greenhorn green tortoise. I simply wasn't sophisticated enough to understand that sellers could care less what a Board of Realtors thinks their members' commissions should be.

Nonetheless, I was excited about my first opportunity to get a shot at earning a jumbo-size commission. I told my Type Number Two professor that I was confident I could find a buyer for his St. Louis apartment development if he would furnish me with the necessary data. I gave him a long list of items I thought I would need in order to put together a proper presentation, and he agreed to have his staff compile the information and get it to me within a week or so.

Now, all I needed was a little something in writing from him and I would be all set. Sadly, however, I was so intimidated by his arrogant, self-righteous attitude that I was very meek in requesting a written understanding regarding my commission. As I verbally stumbled around like the world-class reptilian wimp that I was, he interrupted me and commenced giving me another sanctimonious lecture. He so aggressively emphasized his unparalleled reputation for honesty and integrity that I actually felt ashamed that I had dared to ask for a signed agreement. In the privacy of my mind, I chastised myself for being so disrespectful—for having the gall to ask this paragon of morality for a written agreement. Didn't I realize that when you deal with a man of such unparalleled integrity, you don't need anything in writing?

Clearly, my Type Number Two professor was the intimidator and I was the intimidatee.

Backing off gracefully, I assured him that my asking for an agreement was only a formality, and that in his case I was not concerned about having something in writing. Fluttering my eyelashes in blissful ignorance, I returned to my office and began laying out a game plan to market my first major deal. After my Court Holder experience in organic chemistry class years earlier, I never thought I could become so infatuated again. Young love is beautiful to behold, especially when you spend most of your life hiding inside a shell.

After I received all the facts and figures from my Type Number Two professor's office, I made arrangements to fly to St. Louis to personally inspect his property. There was big money involved, and I was determined to do such a first-class job in all aspects of this deal that the seller would actually feel good about paying me my commission. (Yes, I am blushing a bright shade of green as I write this.)

As quickly as possible, I sent letters to a number of the biggest real estate buyers in the country, briefly describing the St. Louis property and inquiring as to whether they might have an interest in an apartment development of this size. To those who answered in the affirmative, I sent a detailed presentation. Finally, after about two weeks, I followed up with a phone call to each prospect.

One company, in particular, indicated a serious interest in the deal, which resulted in an exchange of numerous phone calls and letters between us. I then made my second critical mistake. (The first, of course, was that I had allowed the seller to intimidate me into believing that I had no need for a signed commission agreement.) Instead of registering the prospective buyer by certified mail, I relayed offers and counter-offers between him and the seller by telephone. During this period, however, I did not mention the buyer's name to the seller.

Then, the inevitable: My professor began to smell the aroma of money and reared his chip-snatching Type Number Two head. He told me he had just returned from New York where he had met with someone who, by coincidence, worked for the buyer with whom I had been negotiating. He said that a mutual acquaintance had introduced him to the buyer, and that the buyer had informed him that he had been negotiating through me for the purchase of his St. Louis apartment development.

In classic Type Number Two fashion, the seller proceeded to tell me that he felt no obligation to me regarding a sale of his

St. Louis property to my buyer, notwithstanding the fact that it was I who had submitted the property to him. The words *honesty* and *integrity* had suddenly disappeared from his vocabulary. True to his species, when the chips were on the table, he dropped his phony, self-righteous verbiage and warned me, in no uncertain terms, that I had better not reach for my chips.

I was stunned, demoralized, and confused. I tried to pull myself together and take a firm stand, but the tougher I got, the nastier my professor became. Finally, I committed one of the most unforgivable sins of deal-making: I began to press. That quickly brought the matter to a head, and from there things got very emotional. With a straight face, my professor argued that he had found out that I had "simply contacted a lot of prospective buyers" and that "anybody could do that." Gee, and here all along I thought that's what a real estate agent was *supposed* to do.

Although it was clear that I had been responsible not only for calling the buyer's attention to the property but for elevating his interest in it, the reality was that I was dealing from a position of weakness. Naïve soul that I was, I had no commission agreement with the seller, nor did I have so much as a certified letter showing that I had registered the buyer with the seller. All I had were the two words the seller had assured me would be all I would ever need—his *honesty* and *integrity*.

It was obvious that tiptoeing was not going to get me anywhere, so I fell back on my ace in the hole that had landed me my first real estate commission—the $6,500 I had received in the Cincinnati deal—and called my attorney into the fray. This time, however, I was dealing with a hard-core Type Number Two, an outrageous flaunter of white hats whose unspoken motto was: Cheating isn't everything, it's the *only* thing!

When my attorney stepped into the picture, the seller and his in-house felon (er ... attorney) shamelessly laid their cards on the table by pointing out the third and most critical mistake I had made in this deal. Not only did I not have a signed commission agreement or a certified mail slip proving that I had registered the buyer with the seller, I was missing the most important legal tool of all: a real estate license in Missouri, the state where the property was located.

The seller's attorney gleefully informed my lawyer and me that, in fact, Missouri had a law *prohibiting* unlicensed persons from working on the sale of properties located within the state. Accordingly, in the event of a sale, a seller had no legal obligation to pay a commission to anyone who did not have a real estate license in Missouri, even if the broker was licensed in another state. My attorney quickly checked it out and confirmed that the seller's attorney was absolutely right.

(This was my first recollection of having an intuitive libertarian thought. The idea that the government had the power to ordain who should and should not be allowed to earn a living selling real estate was instinctively anti-liberty to me. In the coming years, as I became more educated about freedom and free markets, it became obvious why those who are already licensed in any field of endeavor—be they real estate agents, doctors, hair dressers, gambling casinos, or pimps—are almost always in favor of ever tougher licensing laws: It keeps the competition out! In finer circles, it's known as the Government Licensing Scam.)

I assessed the playing field and quickly determined that what I was involved in here was nothing less than a legal mugging—i.e., a mugging backed by a state government. In fact, had I not had the good sense to call in my attorney at the eleventh hour, I would have walked away from this distasteful experience chipless. It was only because of the Universal Attorney-to-Attorney Respect Rule that my Type Number Two professor had his attorney tell my attorney that if I kept my mouth shut and stayed out of the way, he would, in a spirit of generosity, throw me a $20,000 bone. Given that it was going to be a bone or nothing, I chose the bone. While it fell far short of the $200,000+ commission I had expected to receive, it helped me to have an even greater appreciation for the Universal Attorney-to-Attorney Respect Rule and the importance of bringing it into play whenever possible.

My Type Number Two professor at Screw U. had taught me well. I had made one of the biggest apartment-development sales in the history of St. Louis and walked away with but a token fee amounting to about one-fourth of one percent of the selling price of the property. I painstakingly analyzed my mistakes and concluded that in this—my first major deal—I had been missing not one, not two, but all three of the legal tools a real estate agent needs to protect himself.

Because my professor had been such a master craftsman, I felt confident I could spot a Type Number Two pretty quickly in the future. Whenever a person spent an inordinate amount of time expounding on his honesty and integrity, I knew it was a signal for me to pull out my can of roach killer or, preferably, avoid dealing with him at all. I also vowed that if someone refused to sign a commission agreement with me in the future—*regardless* of the reason—I would assume that he was a Type Number Two and walk away from the deal.

As with my organic chemistry class Court Holder many years earlier, I thank you, Type Number Two professor, wherever you may be. I vividly recall your telling me that you would like to do some building in warm weather climates, so I'm sincerely happy for you that you're going to get your wish when you pass on to the next world.

CHAPTER 8

My Senior Year at Screw U.

The St. Louis fiasco I discussed in the previous chapter (officially listed in the Screw U. archives as "the Missouri Massacre") was a major turning point in my career because it forced me to separate reality from wishes—the reality that the game of business is played in a jungle rather than on a nursery school playground; the reality that there are only three types of people in the business world, and that all three are out to get your chips; the reality that I had been dealing from a position of weakness and, as a result, had allowed myself to be intimidated repeatedly.

I vowed that I would find a way to strengthen my posture and that I would begin to earn, and *receive*, big commissions. However, I had not yet determined just how to go about accomplishing my objective. Still reeling from the Missouri Massacre, I needed time to clear my head in order to formulate a workable game plan.

It took a little over a year for me to put the finishing touches on a reality-based philosophy that I could use as a foundation for a winning strategy. While the lessons from the Missouri Massacre were fermenting in my mind, along with those learned from my Type Number One and Type Number Three professors, I needed more experience in learning how to deal with the frustrations and humiliations of the Business World Jungle before I would be prepared to make a significant move up the food chain. My experiences during the next year—my last year at Screw U.—gave me the final preparation I needed.

Three experiences, in particular, stand out in my mind in this regard, experiences that showed me not only how to survive but to come out on top in the wild and woolly Business World Jungle. All three were second-mortgage deals, and in each case the fact that I was dealing from a position of weakness was glaringly apparent to everyone involved. These experiences also underscored for me the inefficiency of working on small deals.

Following are brief accounts of those final three credits that I needed to earn my undergraduate degree from Screw U.

Credit No. 1: Even though I received $20,000 for selling the St. Louis property, things were still pretty tight for me financially, which I increasingly came to realize was at the heart of my problems. It's a difficult problem to hide. My posture was weak precisely because I needed every commission so badly. Even if you're vigilant when it comes to being careful about what you say, your facial expressions, your body language, and the tone of your voice never fail to give you away. And the person you're counting on to pay your fee can· sense your anxiety; you need the money, and he knows it.

Such was the atmosphere at one of my second-mortgage closings that took place shortly after the Missouri Massacre. My Type Number One professor had rejected this particular second-mortgage proposal, so I took it to another lender. The one thing that stands out in my mind about this deal is that I worked harder on it than I did on many of my later closings that resulted in huge commissions, yet I was paid—begrudgingly—a fee of only $1,250 for my services. The critical factor was that I *needed* the $1,250 very badly, and I let it show. As a result, I allowed myself to be intimidated.

I can clearly recall the builder's attorney telling me at the closing, in so many words, that if I was a good boy and kept my mouth shut (shades of St. Louis), I *might* get the $1,250 that was coming to me. As I sat there, humiliated, I felt a great deal of self-disdain for allowing myself to get into another situation where I was completely at the mercy of a principal. I asked myself what errors in judgment I had made that put me in a position to be down on my hands and knees, groveling like a beggar and hoping to be thrown another bone?

Finally, after many sadistic attempts on the part of the borrower's attorney to increase my anxiety level, the $1,250 bone was relinquished. If tortoises could bark, Legalman probably would have made me stand on my haunches and give it a go before tossing me my meager reward. It was one of the most degrading episodes of my undergraduate days at Screw U.

As I sat through the closing, playing the toady role to the hilt and meekly doing whatever I was told, I vowed to rectify my posture in the future so I would never again have to experience such degradation. I was determined to find a way to maneuver myself into a position of strength to the point of being virtually intimidation-proof.

I also made up my mind, right then and there at the execution (er ... closing), that I would work only on deals that had the potential for a payoff big enough to justify my time and effort. Barking was bad enough, but barking for $1,250 was shameful. It was getting near graduation time at Screw U., and I was tired of working on deals to the point of exhaustion, only to end up having to beg for my commissions, most of which were penny ante in size.

"*Down, boy, down. Be good and keep your mouth shut, and I might throw it to you.*"

Credit No. 2: My second credit involved another second-mortgage loan that my Type Number One professor had turned down, so I submitted it to another lender in New York. I made up my mind that I was going to go for a substantial fee in this deal, though I realized I would have to structure it in such a way that the borrower would not feel as though it was coming out of "his" money (shades of my first-ever real estate closing in Cincinnati).

As second mortgages go, it was a large loan request 500,000—but I felt that the collateral was strong enough to support such a loan. The lender seemed to agree, and expressed a serious interest. He sent a representative to inspect the property, after which I flew to New York to meet with the lender personally and see if there was anything I could do to help expedite a closing. At the meeting, I explained that I had quoted the prospective borrower an interest rate in the area of 13 percent plus a front-end "discount" fee of 10 percent.

I also informed the lender that, for psychological reasons, I had told the borrower that he (the lender) would be responsible for paying my fee. I reasoned that if the borrower paid me directly, he would protest my being paid a $15,000 fee (which I had built into the 10 percent up-front discount). However, if my fee was tacked on to the lender's up-front discount—much the same as in my Cincinnati deal—the borrower would think of it as coming out of the lender's pocket rather than his. It was, of course, pure pacification on my part, but I had already learned how important it was to humor borrowers and sellers. When people cry out to be deluded, it's inhumane not to accommodate them—especially if they're sellers or borrowers.

I proceeded to explain to the lender that he needed only a 7 percent discount in order to bring his effective interest rate up to the normal backbreaking levels he was used to extracting from borrowers, and that he could pay me the additional 3 percent discount as my $15,000 fee.

Result? The lender went absolutely berserk! During the ensuing heated discussion, he said two things that would ring in my ears for the remainder of my days at Screw U. First, he said, "You have a lot of nerve trying to earn $15,000 on one deal. I mean, you're *only* a broker." Wham—right between the eyes. Talk about painting a clear picture of how I was perceived by a lender. How could I help but see the light when this killer-lender was shining it right in my eyes? In reality, he was actually doing me a favor by indirectly reminding me just how weak my posture was. I was *only* a broker and therefore had no right to earn $15,000 on one deal. Shame on me for trying to grab more than a petite sliver of the monstrous loan pie.

Of course, it was all right for the lender to charge that much, and more, for such "services" as prepaid interest or "privileges" such as prepayment penalties. Why? Because he had the right posture; he was dealing from a position of strength. One of the fascinating things about the human psyche is that people don't begrudge a wealthy person's making money, but they very much resent someone of lesser means making "too much" money. I had been found guilty of trying to violate one of the most sacred, unwritten rules of the Jungle—the rule that little guys don't have a right to make big money. Marie Antoinette said, "Let them eat cake," which was kind of cute. But this New York lender with a Ho Chi Minh personality went one step further and seemed to be saying, "Let loan brokers eat—but not too much."

The second unbelievable thing the lender said was that it was "unconscionable" for me to charge a 3 percent brokerage fee for the placement of a second-mortgage loan. It was a remarkable statement considering that he was commonly referred to as the Doctor Death of the second-mortgage business. Here was a man who had built his fortune on the misfortune and financial desperation of others, who earned interest rates of 15 percent and more, used hidden-charge gimmicks such as "prepaid interest," "discount fees," and "prepayment penalties" to increase his return, and who was now proclaiming that it was unconscionable for *me* to make $15,000 on one deal. I had visions of the lender's remains sitting on a supermarket shelf, neatly packaged as *Soylent Green*.

*"You have a lot of nerve trying to earn $15,000 on one deal.
Don't you understand that you're only a broker?"*

The Theory of Relativity comes into play here, because relative to the kind of profits the lender was used to making, my fee was insignificant. But relative to the crumbs that loan brokers usually have to settle for, my fee was "unconscionable." It was clear to me that the only way I could ever hope to have my "relativity status" upgraded was to find a way to change my posture. It was a matter of perception, of being thought of as one of those important guys who had a *right* to earn big money.

The deal, as you might have guessed, never closed, because I had dared to step out of line by attempting to earn a meaningful commission—*without being prepared to see it through*. But with graduation time at Screw U. near at hand, I was just about ready to put the final pieces of my reality-based philosophy into place and elevate my posture to a level where it would be difficult for tortoise predators in the Business World Jungle to intimidate me.

Credit No. 3: My final course at Screw U.—the one that tied the ribbon around my diploma—involved a second-mortgage loan on an apartment development in Tampa. Having fulfilled most of my undergraduate requirements, I was experienced enough to be able to quickly spot the warning signs that warned me I would have trouble collecting my fee if the deal closed.

By this time, getting the borrower to sign a fee agreement with me was a given, and I didn't need a real estate license in Florida, because there was no sale involved. I was again shooting for an "unconscionable" fee of $15,000, only this time it was even more unconscionable because it was based on a much smaller loan than the one in my previous deal. Also, this time around, my fee wasn't buried in the lender's front-end discount. I put all my cards on the table from the outset, clearly spelling out in our agreement that I was to receive my fee directly from the borrower.

As things progressed and it began to look like the deal was going to close, I became so certain that the borrower had no intention of paying me my $15,000 fee that I started customizing a plan to protect myself. First, I purposely did not give the borrower any indication that I intended to be present at the closing, because I didn't want him to be on guard. I was pretty certain that it would never occur to him that a loan broker would fly halfway across the country to collect a fee at a closing, because a typical masochist-broker naively waits for his commission check to be mailed to him. (If you ever ventured into a loan broker's or real estate agent's office and were surprised to see a cobweb-covered skeleton—cigar butt between its teeth—sitting behind the desk, you were probably looking at a broker or agent who was waiting for his commission check to arrive.)

I figured that as long as it didn't occur to the borrower that I might attend the closing, he would not focus, in advance, on making certain that I wasn't allowed in the closing room on judgment day. I purposely avoided discussing my commission with him during our many telephone discussions, which must have had him cackling to himself about how easy the upcoming chip theft was going to be.

As it turned out, I actually had a very important appointment scheduled for the same day as the Tampa closing, so, without announcing it to anyone in advance, I sent an assistant to Tampa the night before the loan was to be finalized. I told him to show up at the closing the next morning, be very friendly and matter-of-fact, and present my signed fee agreement to the attorneys representing the borrower and lender. Given that he had a law degree, I felt there was a good chance he could invoke the Universal Attorney-to-Attorney Respect Rule as a way of protecting my fee.

The next evening, my assistant called me long distance to relate what had taken place at the closing. Laughingly, he told me that the borrower had done a double-take when he walked through the door. Then, after a lot of mumbling and stalling, the borrower finally handed over a $15,000 check to him. The bad news, however, was that the check was not certified!

Even though I had had very little sleep over the past several days and was exhausted from having worked without a break since early that morning, the adrenalin started flowing at mach speed when I heard that the check wasn't certified. As early as Jungle 101 you learn that an uncertified check should be viewed as no check at all.

I quickly called the airlines and found that if I hurried, I had just enough time to throw a few things in a bag and make it to the airport for a late-evening flight to Tampa. On top of everything else, I hadn't eaten a thing all day, and I was ravenous. My mental scales instantly weighed the two options. One option was to give in to my hunger and exhaustion and fly to Tampa the next morning—very possibly too late to cash the $15,000 check. The other option was to ignore my hunger and exhaustion and fly to Tampa that night so I could get an early start on protecting my $15,000. Hunger and exhaustion never had a chance.

I grabbed a few necessities, checked to make sure I had some cash, credit cards, and, above all, identification, and jumped in my car. As is always the case with late-evening flights, the trip was miserable, and I arrived in Tampa feeling like a corpse. My assistant met me at the airport, after which time we hurried to the motel where he was staying. I quickly checked in, then sat down to discuss strategy with him.

As you would expect, I always counted heavily on the hare making the mistake of pausing at some point. Maybe he would stop off to have a martini, or eat lunch, or get some other work done, or just put "it" off until tomorrow because it was so late in the day. Whatever the cause might be, I had developed great faith that my opponent would always become lax at some point along the way and give me just enough time to make certain that the Tortoise and Hare Theory took effect. (*If you slow down enough to look over your right shoulder, I'll pass you on the left; if you slow down enough to look over your left shoulder, I'll pass you on the right; etc.*)

My cross-country trip had been based on an assumption and a gamble. The assumption was that the borrower was going to stop payment on the $15,000 check; the gamble was that he would make the mistake of procrastinating and not take care of the matter until the bank opened the next morning.

I grabbed a couple hours of restless sleep at the motel, then dragged myself out of bed at the crack of dawn. I was taking no chances on not being at the front door of the bank when it opened. I felt as though I hadn't slept in a week, but a cold shower and the thought of $15,000 was stimulating enough to keep me moving.

Finally, there I was—black business suit, black-rimmed sunglasses, and black briefcase—standing in front of the bank, waiting for it to open. Needless to say, I was the first customer through the door that morning. I walked directly to a teller's window and presented the $15,000 check for payment. Calmly laying out my personal identification items on the counter, I explained that I would like the $15,000 in cash, with as many large bills as possible (so I could fit it all into my briefcase). It was a scene right out of *Scarface*.

You haven't lived until you've walked into a strange bank, in a faraway town—wearing a black suit, black-rimmed sunglasses, and carrying a black briefcase—and tried to cash a $15,000 check. I think everyone in the bank just assumed that I was connected with the Mafia. Within minutes, a whole cadre of bank employees was buzzing around trying to figure out what to do about this unheard-of request. Someone—a strange someone at that—was actually demanding that a bank come up with real, live cash in place of a check! The nerve of a tortoise to want cash.

A bank officer finally "took charge" and explained that he would have to call the person who had endorsed the check to make certain it was not a forged endorsement. (The check had been disbursed on an attorney's trust account directly to the borrower, and the borrower had then endorsed it over to me.)

I argued that the check was drawn on his bank, that he could examine the attorney's signature on the front of the check to confirm it was valid, and that the only other thing he needed to do was confirm that the funds were in the account. I insisted that there was no reason to involve the endorser. I knew that a call to the borrower/endorser would be an invitation to a dispute that in all likelihood would result in payment on the check being stopped—or at least held up. No luck; the bank officer insisted on making the call.

My wheels started turning again, only faster. I thought to myself that even if the borrower was intending to stop payment on the check, he probably had not had time to think through just how he was going to do it, because it was drawn on the trust account of the attorney representing the lender. After all, he had been taken by surprise when my assistant showed up at the closing. I was further counting on the fact that, like a true hare, he would get sidetracked for a while. I believed there was a reasonable chance that the attorney who had disbursed the money for the lender might not know what the borrower's intentions were (assuming his intentions were, in fact, to try to stop payment on the check).

I quickly blurted out that I thought the endorser of the check had said he would be out of town that day, and that the banker would probably have more success calling the attorney who had originally signed the check. I emphasized the logic of my suggestion by pointing out that the attorney was a customer of the bank. Success! The banker took my suggestion and called the attorney instead. To say the least, Legalman was quite surprised to hear that I was in town, and even more surprised to hear that I was at the bank trying to cash the $15,000 check. Nonetheless, he confirmed that he had signed the check and had watched the borrower endorse it in my name.

Then came "The Scene." It was destined to rank right up there years later with "The Drive" (John Elway), "The Pass" (Joe Montana), and "The Catch" (Dwight Clark). There I was, standing in front of the teller's cage in my black suit and black-rimmed sunglasses, stuffing $15,000 cash into my black briefcase as a security guard dutifully stood by. I was so focused on securing possession of the $15,000 that it was not until I clicked shut the

"$13,100 . . . $13,200 . . . $13,300 . . ."

latches on my bulging briefcase that I noticed everyone in the bank was staring at me.

"Crying all the way to the bank" is an old cliché, but in this case I *laughed* all the way *from* the bank.

I have no way of knowing if it ever came to pass, but the thought that the borrower might have been calling the bank or Legalman to see if there was some way he could stop payment on the check—while I was on my way to the airport carrying a briefcase filled with $15,000 cash—made the nightmare of the previous twelve hours a small price to pay.

On the plane trip home, as I laid back in my seat, thoroughly exhausted, I told myself that the time had arrived. No more crawling around on my hands and knees and no more penny-ante deals. From now on I was going to display a high-level posture, and the money was going to be big. Graduation time at Screw U. had arrived, and my impeccable education had prepared me to go forth into the Business World Jungle and start hunting for big game.

CHAPTER 9

MY GRADUATION FROM SCREW U.

A fter completing my Tampa credit at Screw U., it was time to organize my experiences into a workable, reality-based philosophy, then lay out a specific plan for implementing it. My first major decision in this regard was to switch my efforts from second-mortgage loans to the sale of large commercial properties.

At first I was a bit apprehensive about no longer specializing in second-mortgage loans, because I had worked so hard to learn the business and establish some great contacts. When I finally made the decision, however, the reasoning I used was destined to become an integral part of my thinking for the rest of my life.

That reasoning is encapsulated in the Leapfrog Theory, which states: *No one has an obligation—moral, legal, or otherwise—to*

*"work his way up through the ranks." Every human being pos-
sesses an inalienable right to make a unilateral decision to redi-
rect his career and begin operating on a higher level at any time
that he, and he alone, believes he is ready.*

If one aspires to great accomplishments, he must recognize
that the quickest way to the top is not by fighting his way *through*
the pack, but by leapfrogging *over* it. There is, however, a catch.
If you aren't prepared to rise above the competition, then, in spite
of any bold proclamations, the realities of the Business World
Jungle will knock you right back into the pack in short order. In
other words, even though you have a perfect right to proclaim
that you're ready to move beyond your competitors, no amount
of chest-pounding can overcome reality.

Conversely, the more you're prepared, the better your
chances of staying on the higher level you have unilaterally chosen for yourself. It's enormously frustrating to know in your heart
that you're capable of bigger accomplishments, yet spend most of
your time and energy fighting day-to-day battles in the midst of
rank-and-file mediocrity. But if you're truly prepared to move up
the ladder in your profession, there's no law that requires you to
wait for the conventional-wisdom crowd to anoint you.

In other words, the easiest way to handle your competition
is to simply refuse to acknowledge it. Without seeking anyone's
permission or being saddled by guilt feelings, you simply take
it upon yourself to begin operating on a higher level. You don't
have to wait for industry bigwigs or anyone else to christen you
an expert in your chosen field.

(Interestingly, years after I had written *Winning Through
Intimidation*, a well-known doctor in Los Angeles, who was
married to a famous actress, confided in me that if he had not
read my book and implemented the Leapfrog Theory, he never
would have had the courage to leave his home town, move to Los
Angeles, and become a "celebrity" doctor.)

Likewise, had I not implemented the Leapfrog Theory, I
probably would still be begging for crumbs begrudgingly tossed to

me by unappreciative second-mortgage borrowers. Instead, I was able to receive, less than five months later, a sales commission almost twice the combined total of all the commissions I had received during my first three years in the real estate business.

Once I made the decision to put the Leapfrog Theory into action, I analyzed my most memorable experiences prior to and during my years at Screw U., extracted the lessons learned from them, and worked on putting everything I had learned into a workable philosophy. Most of this was accomplished sitting on a big rock next to a river, thinking and taking notes. And the more I thought, the more I became convinced that intimidation had been at the root of most of my problems when it came to being short-chipped in the deals I had worked on. Recognizing this fact motivated me to devise and implement specific techniques to protect myself against the kinds of intimidators who had bludgeoned me in the past.

In fact, I became convinced, and still am, that the problems most people encounter in trying to achieve their objectives—in business, personal relationships, and virtually all other areas of their lives—stem from being intimidated by others. For real estate agents, the intimidation comes from both buyers and sellers (or, in the case of second-mortgage loans, borrowers and lenders). But regardless of one's business, the problem is the same—being intimidated into allowing others to control your destiny.

Stated in theory form, what I'm talking about here is the Theory of Intimidation, which states: *The results a person achieves are inversely proportionate to the degree to which he is intimidated.*

Clearly, it was in the deals in which I had been intimidated the most that I had taken the greatest financial beatings, and it was in the deals in which I had been intimidated the least that I had walked away with the greatest number of chips.

While I felt confident that I had zeroed in on the crux of the problem, doing something about it was another matter altogether. The first step toward solving a problem is to analyze its causes. Why and how had I been cast in the role of the intimidatee in past dealings? I felt confident that I had more knowledge and ability than most of the principals with whom I had dealt, but knowledge and ability seemed to have no effect on our respective positions as intimidator and intimidatee.

Based on firsthand experience, it was apparent to me that the most relevant factor in my ongoing dilemma was my *posture*, a conclusion that produced the Posture Theory, which states: *It's not what you say or do that counts, but what your posture is when you say or do it.*

In real estate brokerage, for example, if your posture suggests that you're "only a broker" (to borrow the words of the second-mortgage lender who believed that my fee was "unconscionable"), and the principals see you as nothing more than an unnecessary annoyance in their deal, you're going to end up being intimidated no matter how great your knowledge and ability and no matter how impressive your words and actions are.

So, in my mind, the overriding question became: What can I do to improve my weak posture? I was clear to me that I had to figure out a way to maneuver myself into a position of (apparent) power. When I thought about power, I couldn't help but recall my old Type Number One professor in the second-mortgage business who was the epitome of someone whose posture was impenetrable. At the heart of his posture power was wealth, which was evident to prospective borrowers without his ever having to utter a word.

However, I also recalled a number of people whom I had known to be respected—even feared—who played the game from a position of strength, notwithstanding their lack of wealth. Obviously, these people had something else going for them that had nothing to do with money, something that resulted in a powerful image. In cases like these, I concluded that it was a matter of perception overriding reality. In life in general, when it comes to substance versus perception, I'll almost always opt for substance. But, like it or not, a harsh reality of the Jungle is that perception can often carry the day. And up to this point in my career, perception had done an excellent job of consistently separating me from my chips.

The only practical solution was that I could no longer operate as "only a broker." I had to portray an image that would change the perception of principals in the deals I worked on. They would have to respect me enough to feel that I had a *right* to earn big commissions. It was a silly head game, but I recognized I would have to learn to play it, and play it well, if I intended to survive in the Jungle.

I also recognized that it was necessary to possess a certain amount of *real* power if I didn't want to come across as the emperor with no clothes. In other words, I didn't want to rely solely on image without having something to back it up. Substance *is* important. And, based on my Cincinnati and St. Louis experiences, I recognized that one of the most substantive things I could do was to have *legal* strength. I was convinced that if I had the proper legal tools on my side, it would give me the real power I needed.

During my years at Screw U., I had become ever more careful about having all my t's crossed and i's dotted. I had learned, to my delight, that whenever I brought my attorney into a deal, the Universal Attorney-to-Attorney Respect Rule came into play and gave me the power I needed to keep from being cannibalized. I reasoned that if both my legal power and image power were strong from the outset, they would, in turn, give me the posture to having *staying* power.

The key to legal power was to use my own past disastrous experiences as a guide to developing the proper legal tools. I had flunked enough tests at Screw U. to be able to recognize that there were basically three critical legal tools at the disposal of any real estate agent who had the courage and determination to employ them.

The first tool was now obvious to me—a real estate license in the state where the property was located. No matter how offended one may be at a state government's standing in the way of his selling real estate without its approval, the reality is that it's the way the world works. That being the case, I accepted this reality and pledged that I would be licensed in every state in which I wanted to sell property. It involved a considerable amount of time, energy, and investment, but I ultimately obtained real estate licenses in eleven states and the District of Columbia at a time when multi-state licensing in real estate was virtually unheard of. (As it turned out, I preceded Century 21 Real Estate by several years as a nationwide real estate brokerage firm.)

The second legal tool was a signed commission agreement with the seller before beginning to work on his property. Experience had taught me that it was nothing short of suicide to work on a deal on the basis of a verbal understanding. As a graduating senior at Screw U., I was truly amazed at how many real estate agents worked on the sale of large properties without having a written commission agreement with the seller. No matter how many times many real estate agents are victimized, they can't seem to come to grips with the reality that it is normally not in the seller's best interest to see them receive a big commission— or any commission at all!

I had already become pretty successful at securing signed commission agreements from borrowers and sellers, but "pretty successful" would no longer be satisfactory. I vowed that in the future, no matter how good the deal or how big the potential commission, I would not expend an ounce of energy until the seller signed a commission agreement.

The third legal tool was the use of certified mail. (Obviously, there was no such thing as e-mail at that time.) At Screw U., I had observed that whenever I used certified mail to submit a deal to a lender or buyer, then registered the name of the lender or buyer with the borrower or seller, the principals were far less likely to ignore me. As a result of using certified mail, they were aware that if a lawsuit were to develop over my commission, the introduction of dated and stamped certified slips and letters into court proceedings would be strong evidence of my degree of involvement. I had already been using certified mail sporadically for quite some time, but now I laid out a system of certified-mail communication that was so intricate that I felt confident it would practically prove my case in court if I ever had to file suit to collect a commission.

It's important to point out, however, that while these legal tools could be very effective in cases where litigation became necessary, their primary purpose was to help me *avoid* litigation. It was my version of a Star Wars defense shield: I wasn't out to attack anyone; I just wanted to make it as difficult as possible for some unscrupulous principal to launch an intercontinental ballistic axe aimed at my fingers.

With the techniques I describe in the next chapter, I finally achieved the *image power* I had dreamed about for so long. And with the use of my three legal tools, I would have the *real power* to back up my new image. But I wanted to take it one step further and back up my image power and legal power by being the best at my profession. In other words, I wanted to demonstrate *performance power*. There is nothing more powerful than having a reputation for getting results. The combination of image *and* substance is virtually unbeatable, and that was my aim.

Legal power is essential in the Jungle, but from a self-esteem standpoint, performance power is a real high. Nothing beats the feeling, in your heart of hearts, of knowing that you really do deserve to be handsomely rewarded because you provided great value to the party you represented. I wanted to make it as difficult as possible for a seller to pass the giggle test if he claimed I had not earned my commission. From now on, it was going to be obvious to both the buyer and seller that the initiation, progress, and conclusion of the sale were due primarily to the efforts of The Tortoise.

The Theory of Intimidation and the Posture Theory put the finishing touches on the reality-based philosophy I had been developing for years, both prior to and during my undergraduate days at Screw U. I now believed I had the education and experience to apply my philosophy not only to the earning *and* receiving of large real estate commissions, but to every aspect of life. There was no question about it, majoring in Reality at Screw U. was the smartest thing I ever did.

At long last, my philosophy was not only clearly developed, but organized in such a way that it was practical to use in my day-to-day dealings. It was no longer theory, but reality. I had succeeded in extracting the lessons learned from my painful experiences at Screw U. and converting them into a workable philosophy. All that remained was for me to customize my techniques to fit each new situation and thereby rearrange the division of the chips in the deals I worked on.

You might say that it was my customized version of a redistribution-of-the-wealth program. In the past, I had often been aware of the right thing to do, but had allowed my emotions to overrule my intellect. As part of my plan to change my image, I would now place great emphasis on allowing my intellect to guide my actions and thereby elevate my status in the Business World Jungle.

I also recognized that once I proclaimed myself to be above the pack—i.e., announced to the world that I had leapfrogged to a new level—I would be the target of much derision, even outrage. Having developed a pretty good understanding of human nature at Screw U., there was little doubt in my mind that my audacious decision to leapfrog over my peers in the real estate business was an almost certain invitation to jealousy, resentment, and scorn.

How did I summon the courage to move forward in the face of such certain discomfort? Easy. I just kept thinking about the excruciating pain I had suffered on so many occasions at Screw U. and concluded that a little jealousy, resentment, and scorn was a small price to pay in return for dignity, peace of mind, and financial success. Being liked was not much of a reward for being poor and disrespected. By the same token, money and respect were more than enough consolation for having a pack of insecure neurotics dislike me.

In the next five chapters, I discuss what I believe to be the five basic steps of selling. From the outset, I want to emphasize that these steps can be applied to virtually any aspect of life. It's more than just a trite statement to say that we sell ourselves to the rest of the world every day of our lives. Whether or not you like it, you *are* a salesman, both in your business and personal life.

The first four steps of selling are familiar to most people. Being a successful salesman requires:

1. Having a product to sell that other people value.

2. Locating a market (i.e., buyers) for your product.

3. Implementing a sales presentation and/or marketing strategy.

4. Closing the sale.

These four steps have been discussed in many sales books, but, remarkably, I've never seen the fifth—and most important—step discussed in any book:

5. GETTING PAID!

The above two words are the only ones in this book that I have both capitalized and underlined, which should give you a good idea of the degree of importance I place on getting paid. Throughout the book I have continually used the phrase *earning and receiving*. Why do I keep adding the words "and receiving?" Because, as everyone who has ever tried to sell anything has discovered, to his dismay, it's one thing to earn a fee, but quite another to actually *receive* it. You make a grave mistake if you develop the habit of prematurely celebrating.

Think of it as the Bottom-Line Theory, which states: *You're not through until you've crossed all the t's, dotted all the i's, and the check has cleared the bank. Everything else is fluff.*

In the remainder of this book, it will become obvious to you that the techniques I used to satisfy the first four selling steps were oriented toward successfully completing the fifth and most important step: *getting paid.*

I again emphasize that the philosophy I used can be applied not only to any other kind of business, but to one's personal life as well. It's just a matter of customization; reality applies to all areas of life. Regardless of what it is you're trying to accomplish, always ask yourself: What must I do to bring about the payoff I'm after?

It was a long and agonizing road I had traveled, a road lined with endless frustration, humiliation, and pain. But The Tortoise had responded by doing what he is programmed to do from birth—plodding and trudging forward in the hopes of somehow finding a way to cross the finish line before the hare awakens.

Now, lo and behold, the time had come for The Tortoise to graduate from Screw U. The moment had arrived for him to move deep into the foreboding interior of the Business World Jungle and begin playing the game for big chips. The $1 blackjack table no longer excited him. Swing open the doors to the baccarat room and make way for The Tortoise! (If you're going to mix metaphors, you can't do better than *foreboding interior of the Business World Jungle* and *swing open the doors to the baccarat room.* Hmmm.)

I felt that if I was right about my philosophy, it should result in my earning, *and* receiving, substantial real estate commissions on a regular basis.

As I stood at the gates of Screw U. for the last time, I looked back at my three professors who were observing my departure with varying degrees of curiosity. With arms spread and raised above my head, each hand displaying the traditional Nixonian victory sign, I smiled warmly and declared, "Let me make one thing perfectly clear: You won't have The Tortoise to kick around anymore."

With that, I turned and made my final exit through the magnificent, blood-stained gates of Screw U., humming the school's alma mater as I disappeared into the Business World Jungle in search of bigger game.

*"Let me make one thing perfectly clear: You won't have
The Tortoise to kick around anymore."*

CHAPTER 10

USING POSTURE POWER
TO GET THE BALL

When it came to obtaining a product to sell, rule number one was to avoid working with other real estate agents—or, as they say in the trade, co-brokering. Experience had taught me that the worst possible way to find deals was through other brokers and salesmen.

Nonetheless, co-brokering seemed to be a way of life for most real estate agents. Rather than spending the time, energy, and money necessary to solicit listings directly from principals, they preferred to take the easy way out and work on deals passed along to them by their peers. One of the main problems with this modus operandi is that you're too far removed from the person who is supposed to pay the commission, which in turn dramatically decreases your chances of getting paid. I felt that an agent who operated in this manner was kidding himself by not confronting head on the Type Number Ones, Twos, and Threes who must ultimately be reckoned with in every sale if a commission is to be paid.

I had known many real estate agents who spent day after day discussing multimillion-dollar deals with other agents, seemingly achieving fulfillment from their conversations alone. They steered clear of the excruciating effort it takes to secure a listing directly from a seller, let alone the time and energy it requires to locate a buyer for a property, implement a marketing method, and close the sale.

Such an agent limits his efforts to sending out tenth-generation copies of scanty information about properties furnished him by other agents. It's a lottery mentality—hoping upon hope that some agent with whom he is dealing will somehow get lucky and close a sale—and then, the ultimate hope, a small piece of the commission will miraculously filter its way down to him.

I'm not saying that a real estate agent should never work with another broker or salesman under any circumstances. That would be ideal, but not practical. Circumstances regarding two of the sales I discuss later in this book were such that it made sense for me to pay a co-brokerage fee to another agent. Even in those instances, however, I took matters into my own hands and did everything possible to control the destiny of the sale.

As a regular habit, however, co-brokering is the best way I know of to decrease your chances of receiving a commission, which is why it should be avoided whenever possible. In simple terms, the shortest distance between two points is a straight line, and when you co-broker a deal, you in effect form a triangle. The odds against closing a major deal are staggering even when you work directly with a principal. But to try to close a sale under the handicap of a third party standing between you and the person who has the power to say *yes* or *no* is nothing short of masochism.

My main interest now was in large apartment developments, and the rule I laid down for myself was to not work on any project that was smaller than 100 units. As I progressed, I increased that minimum to 200 units, but was primarily interested in 300 units and up.

When calling an owner cold, the first thing I wanted to find out was whether or not he had a genuine interest in selling his property. When I phoned for the first time, I made it a point to introduce myself to the owner's secretary before she asked who I was, and then, in a matter-of-fact tone, I said that I wanted to speak to the owner about a "personal matter." The object was to posture myself in such a way as to cause the secretary to assume I knew the owner personally, which I accomplished by volunteering my name rather than waiting for her to ask.

If the secretary still insisted on knowing the nature of my call, I came right out and told her that it regarded the *purchase* (not listing!) of one of her employer's apartment developments. By wording it this way, I assumed that if the owner, after knowing the nature of my call, did not come to the phone, or at least return my call, he wasn't seriously interested in selling his property.

If the owner did not return my call, or if he came to the phone and told me that he had no interest in selling, I would file his name and number in my tickler system for follow-up at a later date. I would then call him back in six months or so to see if circumstances had changed and if he might then have an interest in selling his property. At Screw U. I had learned that most apartment developers have a building disorder—i.e., they are ready and willing, if not able, to build anything, anywhere, anytime—and the more they build, the more financial problems they create for themselves. Which means that circumstances are always changing—especially in the world of real estate developers.

The reason most builders frantically lunge from one project to another is to try to keep enough cash circulating (forget about profits) to pay for the last "I can finance out" deal—which, of course, ended up *not* financing out. A real estate developer with a true building disorder would not hesitate to construct a luxury high-rise in the Australian Outback if he could obtain financing

"What a location, mate.
This project is a guaranteed winner."

for it. In case you're a medical buff, it may interest you to know that in the psychiatric world the term *building disorder* is almost always used in conjunction with its sister term, *pathological builder*. But for our purposes here, let it suffice to say that crazy is crazy no matter how it's phrased.

The owner I was searching for was the guy who would come to the phone and give at least some indication that he might be interested in selling his property. I say *indication*, because an owner will rarely come right out and *admit* that he's interested in selling his property. Experience had taught me that even in cases where an owner was actively trying to sell his property, he would almost always act coy during my initial conversation with him. I ultimately became savvy enough to recognize that when an owner said something like, "I've never really given it much thought," he was, in fact, a serious seller.

Builder-owners bless their hearts, are a unique species. Not only do they not necessarily mean what they say, most of the time they don't even mean what they think they mean. They live in an entirely different world from the rest of us—one that revolves almost entirely around "the next deal"—and they speak a language all their own. By now, though, I had learned to translate "builderese" doublespeak into English pretty well. For example, "I'm always willing to listen" more often than not really meant, "I'm desperate. Make me an offer."

Once the owner displayed an interest in selling, the next step was to obtain some figures about his property so I could determine whether or not a deal was makeable. However, I never asked the owner for this information during my initial conversation with him, because I first wanted to establish my posture. Screw U. had taught me that one of the first things a seller does to ensconce himself as the intimidator is to make the real estate agent justify his existence. Once the seller blurted out something like, "Who are you?" my posture as El Schlepo Tortoise would be forever stamped on his forebrain. No matter how I responded to such an inquiry, I would come across as "just another real estate agent," and an owner needs another real estate agent about as much as he needs another vacant apartment.

So my whole approach was geared to establishing image power in an effort to avoid having to justify my existence. As per the Leapfrog Theory, I not only had to be above being "just another real estate agent," I had to be beyond even being asked who I was. I had to be so far above the rest of the pack that the owner would be too intimidated to dare to ask me such a question.

I accomplished this by having a unique calling card designed. In addition to eliminating the question of who I was, my calling card made it almost impossible for an owner to forget me. That way, even if he wasn't interested in selling his property right now, the chances were pretty good that he would contact The Tortoise down the road if his circumstances changed.

My calling card was a spectacular, full-color, hardcover brochure costing nearly $5 a copy. The black cover had a high-gloss finish, and the brochure opened from bottom to top rather than the more traditional right-to-left format. Centered on the glossy, black front cover was a breathtaking, full-color photo of the earth as seen from one of the Apollo spaceships. Not only was my name not displayed on the front cover, it did not even appear on the inside of the front cover or on the first page.

In fact, all that appeared on the inside front cover were the following words:

Earth
To Life .... Support
To the Explorer .... A Base
To the Wise .... An Investment

On the first page opposite the inside cover was a telescopic view looking down on downtown Chicago. By the time the brochure finally got around to mentioning my name on the following page, there was not much else that needed to be said. Obviously, anyone who used a spectacular $5 brochure as his calling card must be *somebody*. Obviously, anyone who didn't feel it was necessary to even mention his name on the front cover or first two pages of his own brochure must be *somebody*. I was overwhelmed by my own modesty.

The remainder of the brochure consisted primarily of brief statements alluding to my general expertise in the real estate industry. Primarily, though, it contained an abundance of dramatic pictures, logos, maps, and other carefully selected items that didn't have any real meaning, but made it obvious who I was: *Somebody!*

In short, the brochure was intimidating.

It wasn't that people understood what I did for a living after reading the brochure; they just knew that I wasn't simply another member of the pack—not just another real estate agent. The bottom line was that I no longer had to justify my existence to an owner. Rarely did anyone ask me to explain anything more about my background after receiving the Earth brochure. Best of all, because of its spectacular nature, the recipient of the brochure was unlikely to throw it away. It would have been like throwing away a beautifully illustrated hardcover book. Many recipients kept it right on their desks as a conversation piece, or, at the very least, somewhere close by where they could quickly pull it out and show it to visitors.

Before the owner of a property could ask me any questions about my background when we first spoke over the phone, I took the initiative and suggested that I send him some information about myself. Not asking him for any of the details of his property immediately separated me from the rest of the pack, because it was the antithesis of how a real estate agent normally interacts with an owner.

Instead of stuttering and stammering like most real estate agents in an effort to justify my existence to the principal, my strategy was to act nonchalant. The aura I conveyed was that no one deal was that important to me. I even suggested that it would be a good idea for the owner to learn something about me before proceeding further, which was the clincher. Obviously, I wasn't a real estate agent, because real estate agents didn't talk this way.

After mailing my brochure to the owner, I would wait a week or so before calling him again, and when I did call I was usually put right through to him. It was posture power in action! After the unusual nature of my initial telephone inquiry, followed by the arrival of my spectacular calling card, the casting of the roles in the saga was beginning to change. I was well on my way to becoming the intimidator, while giving the owner a long-overdue, well-deserved opportunity to audition for the role of intimidatee. Words can't express just how happy I was for him to have the opportunity to play such a foreign role.

Now I was in an excellent position to further qualify the owner of the property by asking him to relate to me the most pertinent facts over the phone. I developed a formula for calculating, in a matter of seconds, what a property might be worth to a sophisticated buyer. If you want to work on large deals, regardless of the business you're in, it's critical that that you come to grips with the reality that the chances of any specific deal closing—even when the figures make sense—are very slim. (In this regard, it's critical to never lose sight of the Theory of Next.)

But if the mathematics of a deal are completely out of touch with reality, the odds of its leading to a closing hover around zero. With this in mind, I became ever more selective about the properties I worked on. The bottom line was that I was not just interested in finding out whether or not the owner wanted to sell his property. I wanted to find out if the property was *saleable*. It didn't take a Ph.D. from Screw U. to recognize early on that time was the most valuable commodity I possessed.

Think of it as the Makeable-Deal Theory, which states: *Concentrate your efforts on finding a few makeable deals rather than working on a large number of unmakeable deals and clinging to the desperate hope that one of them will miraculously close.*

Realizing the efficacy of this theory, I focused on efficiency. Specifically, I focused on finding that one good deal that had a serious chance of closing rather than working on thirty bad deals and clinging to the hope that luck and the law of averages would sooner or later combine to bring about a closing. Forget luck. Stupidity not only has a way of stifling good luck, it can also skew the law of averages to the detriment of the mentally challenged individual.

Nevertheless, salesmen and entrepreneurs in every industry seem to have a death wish when it comes to working on pie-in-the-sky deals that have virtually no chance of closing. In real estate, I found that owners have an uncanny ability to keep real estate agents hooked on the fantasy that unmakeable deals can somehow be made.

At Screw U. I finally recognized that the makeability of a deal revolved primarily around cash flow (i.e., the cash that's left over after deduction of all expenses and mortgage payments from gross receipts), also commonly referred to as "net spendable." Anyone who has worked extensively with professional real estate buyers understands that cash flow is the name of the game.

Contrary to popular belief, most professional buyers do not look at "tax loss" as a primary consideration when purchasing properties. Myths about the depreciation factor in real estate deals have been perpetuated over the years—primarily by property owners—but the truth of the matter is that most buyers look at tax benefits as a bonus. Cash flow has, is, and almost certainly always will be the most important factor when it comes to valuing income-producing properties—which is why they're called *income-producing* in the first place.

Accordingly, whenever an owner spent a great deal of time talking about the tax-shelter aspects of his property, I mentally rolled my eyes skyward, because I knew it was a sign that he probably did not have a saleable deal. Sort of like criminal defense attorneys who, when short on facts, focus instead on fluff (aka "The O.J. Factor"). Experience had taught me that when an owner's property demonstrated a healthy cash flow, he would be quick to emphasize that fact above all others.

Another early giveaway to an unsaleable property was when an owner put a great deal of emphasis on how much it had cost him to develop the property or how well it was constructed, the two of which usually go hand in hand. The only time the quality of construction was important was when it was so shoddy that it might be viewed as a *negative*. Professional buyers give sellers very little, if any, credit for being dumb enough to overbuild. The hard reality is that the market value of a property, being pretty much based on cash flow, bears little relation to the owner's cost of construction.

Price and value are two entirely different issues. The seller will always take his cost of construction into account when coming up with an asking *price*, but the *value* the buyer places on the property is based primarily on cash flow. If an owner overspends on construction, that's his problem, not the buyer's.

All this led me to the conclusion that the person who knew the *least* about a property's true market value was the owner. Nevertheless, I still needed to get an indication of the owner's asking price, even though I only considered it to be a starting point. I knew (though I never let on) that the price he initially quoted me would be much higher than the price he would ultimately be willing to accept.

I don't recall ever dealing with a serious seller who stuck to his original asking price to the bitter end. Even if a seller really believed that he wasn't going to budge from his original asking price, he always ended up compromising once he smelled the unmistakable aroma of chips on the table—especially if he had financial problems (which was almost always the case).

Speaking of financial problems, that was another critical factor in my determination of whether or not a deal was makeable. Early in every negotiation, I tried to assess the owner's level of desperation, and that's where my ability to translate builderese doublespeak into English came in handy. The reality was that the more desperate the owner, the better my chances of concluding a sale. As a result of my new posture, desperation had become my best friend. Thus, if the owner's asking price was at least within shouting distance of the ball-park price I had calculated, and assuming there were no extraordinarily negative factors involved, I would be prepared to move forward with trying to find a buyer.

Unfortunately, a significant number of properties were not saleable at *any* price, because my calculations showed that most properties had little or no cash flow. In fact, in many instances the properties actually had negative cash flows. Nonetheless, I never met an owner who *admitted* that his property didn't have a positive cash flow. The discrepancy between the owner's math and reality was caused either by his unrealistic projections or by operating statements that conveniently failed to list all expenses—especially replacement costs.

Owners are so unrealistic when it comes to vacancy factors, replacement costs, and other expense items that are not readily ascertainable that I pretty much considered their projections and operating statements to be useless. Instead, I relied on my own calculations, and was able to quickly determine—while talking to the owner on the phone—whether or not his property was saleable. (The lesson to be extracted and used in other areas of one's life is that people are generally unrealistic about most things, particularly when touting their own deals, products, and prospects. Which is why you have to take most of what you hear with a grain of salt, take matters into your own hands, and do your homework.)

If there was little or no cash flow—or, worse, a negative cash flow—or if the owner's asking price was light years beyond the high end of my estimate of the property's value, I bid him adieu and allowed him to go merrily on his way talking to other real estate agents about how much his project had cost to build or what a great tax-loss vehicle it provided.

However, if the mathematics fell within my value parameters, I then told the owner that I would have to personally inspect his property "before making any commitments." With this latter statement, I had managed, for the third time, to set the stage for recasting the roles of intimidator and intimidatee before the owner and I had even met. I could not possibly be a real estate agent, because there was no such thing as a real estate agent who was reluctant to "make a commitment." A normal real estate agent works on *any* deal!

Step one in this role-reversal game had been when I had initially called the owner and suggested that I send him some information about myself before discussing his property in detail. Step two had been when he received the Earth brochure from me. Now, in step three, I was telling him that I was going to board an airplane, at my own expense, and personally inspect his property—and that I could not "make a commitment" until I had completed my inspection. Clearly, I must be "somebody," because it would be unheard of for a lowly real estate agent to talk and act in such a manner.

So when I reached the point not just of finding an owner who was interested in selling his property, but who had a *saleable* property, my next step was to haul my healthy posture onto a plane and pay a personal visit to that owner. Only then could I decide whether or not I would be willing to "make a commitment." Of course, the *real* purpose of my trip was to obtain a signed commission agreement, but how many owners do you think would have been excited about my visiting them had I told them what my real objective was? Zero is a pretty good guess.

To help me be vigilant about sticking to my vow to never again work on a deal without a signed commission agreement, I carried around a little card containing the words of a poem—a true literary masterpiece—I had composed:

With a written agreement,
You have a prayer;
With a verbal agreement,
You have nothing but air.

It has been a source of lasting irritation to me that I was not nominated for a Nobel Prize in Literature for this gem—but, hey, you can't have it all.

Anyone can work on the sale of a property—the more the merrier as far as an owner is concerned, because it increases his chances of making a sale at or near his asking price—but to have a written authorization to do so, an authorization that clearly spells out the agent's commission, is quite another matter.

When I visited the owner's city, the big moment had finally arrived—but with a new twist: It was the big moment for the *owner*, not me. After already having been intimidated no less than three times from long-distance range, he was about to meet a real, live tortoise—not just any old tortoise, but *The* Tortoise. In addition to the image I had taken such great pains to cultivate, I also found that people were more impressed with someone from a distant city than they were with an expert who was readily available to them in their own town. It seemed as though the greater the distance I traveled to visit an owner, the more of an expert I became. What a delightful delusion I had helped plant in the owner's mind. Finally, he was going to be blessed with the opportunity to meet the expert from afar.

When I arrived in the owner's city, I brought with me the equivalent of a portable office, because I made it a point to assume the worst. I assumed, for example, that the owner did not own a decent calculator. I assumed that he used a manual typewriter from out of the fifties. I assumed that he didn't have a functional copier. (Remember, we're talking Stone Age America here.) And, of course, I assumed that his secretary would become hostile if I pressed her to retype something. And, more often than not, most of my assumptions proved to be pretty accurate.

I not only brought my own calculators, typewriters, typing paper, and other supplies and equipment, I also traveled with at least one, and sometimes two or more, secretaries, depending upon the size of the deal.

If you're up to a mental orgasm, picture the setting: Here was a real estate developer who had long delighted in such knee-slapping pastimes as pounding bamboo shoots under real estate agents' fingernails, throwing bones in the middle of a group of ten or twelve starving co-brokers, and engaging in any number of other equally enjoyable kick-the-real-estate-agent torture games. Now, at long last, he sat in his office waiting for his first big meeting with the expert from afar. And rest assured that after such a long wait, I had no intention of disappointing him.

I marched into his office, impeccably dressed in my board chairman's uniform (black pin-stripe suit, white shirt, and black tie with the words "John D. Rockefeller" subliminally woven through it)—black briefcase in hand—followed by an entourage of anywhere from one to three assistants carrying calculators, extension cords, mortgage-rate books, and a variety of other materials and equipment that might be needed.

As you might have guessed, from that point on I was usually in complete control of the situation. While my main reason for bringing my traveling office with me was to make certain that nothing was left to chance, there was a bonus to my road show in that it elevated my posture yet another notch. What really carried the day for me was that I was actually able to pull it off without cracking a smile, notwithstanding the fact that I was chuckling inside.

Once we got down to business, I played the noncommittal role to the hilt, having learned its intricacies from my Type Number One professor at Screw U. I was in no hurry. I had to examine all the figures and look the development over carefully before I could give any indication of my interest or lack thereof. By this time, the owner was usually hyperventilating and salivating simultaneously—a deadly combination that has the potential to make pathological builders an extinct species.

My property-inspection performance was carried out in convincing style. It consisted of strolling through the project and engaging in such stimulating activities as staring at bricks, gingerly tapping walls with my knuckles, and sticking my head down garbage disposals—all the while shaking my head from side to side to imply that I was very concerned about what I was seeing. In other words, I played along with the illusion that these

"Greetings. I've come from afar to inspect your property."

aspects of a property were important to experts. The reality, of course, is that the physical aspects of a property are, at best, of secondary importance to buyers (unless, as previously noted, the quality of construction is so poor that future replacement costs promise to be inordinately high).

Again, the critical factor was cash flow, and I had already roughly calculated it—in a matter of seconds—in my office. Even if the development was built like Fort Knox, I knew it would have little or no effect on the cash-flow numbers. The only significance that exceptionally good construction or other secondary factors might have was that they could possibly nudge a prospective buyer a bit toward the high end of his valuation range, *provided* he was first interested on a cash-flow basis. Nonetheless, I dutifully played out my inspector role, because I knew it was important to give the owner exactly what he was expecting. The last thing in the world I wanted was to be responsible for bursting his delusive little inspection bubble. Always remember that people have a right to delude themselves.

After the inspection, I would sit down with the owner and review as many other largely irrelevant aspects of his property as he expressed a desire to discuss. Finally, when all the meaningless factors had been reviewed to his satisfaction, I zeroed in on the only factor that was relevant: the numbers. This required me to play the role of a surgeon, but instead of asking my assistants for syringes, gauze, and scissors, I had them vigorously slap mortgage-rate books, scratch pads, and pens into my hand on cue. Occasionally, out of the corner of my eye, I would catch a glimpse of the owner's awed expression as I reached out my hand, without looking up, and solemnly commanded, "Red pen!" Voila! The red pen instantly appeared in my hand. It was almost as much fun as getting paid. (Well, not *that* much fun.)

After intensely pounding away on my laptop-sized portable calculator and feverishly thumbing through rate tables, I would finally look up and utter hopeful words such as, "I might be able to do something with this property at around 'X' dollars above the mortgage." I was careful never to say that I could *sell* the property. That would have been too direct. "Might be able to do something" was much more mysterious, and kept the owner on the edge of his mental seat. While they mean essentially the same thing, phrasing, as I pointed out earlier, is of great psychological importance in all aspects of life. Saying that I could *sell* his property would have made me sound like just another real estate agent, but phrasing it the way I did allowed me to maintain my posture as the mysterious expert from afar.

The first figure I threw out to the owner was, of course, always at the low end of what I had calculated to be the broad market range, so I knew in advance that I would get a negative response. My motive, however, was to jolt the owner into coming down considerably from his original, almost always unrealistic, asking price that he had quoted me over the phone.

After the owner countered with a lower figure than his original one, I would then shake my head slowly from side to side, mumble some unintelligible words, open my rate books once again, and start punching away on my calculator. Many mumbles later, I would look up and say something like, "Hmmm ... well, maybe I could stretch that to 'Y' dollars." I jockeyed around like this with the owner until I felt I had gotten the price down as low as I could possibly hope to get it at that early stage of the game. My main objective was to get the owner into the water. Once that was accomplished, I felt confident that the natural flow of events would continually shave the price downward.

I then whipped out my file of pre-typed contracts (which I *never* referred to as contracts, for reasons you should by now understand) and said, in a matter-of-fact tone, something to the effect of, "I like to keep things simple, so I just use a one-page 'understanding' to summarize the deals I'm involved in." Here again it was a matter of word choice. Whether a document is called a *contract* or *understanding* has no legal significance whatsoever, but psychologically it can make all the difference in the world to the person sitting on the other side of the table. Contracts scare people; "understandings" sound innocuous, especially if their purported purpose is only to "summarize the deal." This was a delicate and critical moment for me, because if I failed to get the owner to sign the understanding, I had wasted a lot of time, energy, and money.

Up to that point, I had relied on my image power to support my posture. Now, I needed real power in the form of a legally binding document in order to maintain my strong posture. I considered this to be such a critical step that I took the trouble to develop, over a period of time, a complete series of "understandings" in an attempt to cover nearly every conceivable kind of situation. I did not use an attorney to help me construct these understandings, for two reasons.

First, I did not want my understandings to look too legal. Lengthy, complicated-looking documents—particularly ones containing a lot of legalese—tend to make people back away. If a document was too legal looking, the owner might want to bring in *his* attorney to review it. And once Legalman stepped into the picture, I knew from past experience that I may as well pack up my rate books, calculators, and secretaries, and return from whence I came.

In fact, I went into every deal assuming there was a deal-killing attorney waiting in the wings. While I knew that I would have to come face-to-face with Legalman if and when it came time for a closing to occur, there was no way that I wanted to go up against a master problem-finder before I even had a commission agreement signed.

The second reason I wrote my own understandings was that I wanted to make them as practical as they were legal. Practical Law is not taught at Stanford, Harvard, or any of the other prestigious law schools. It is offered only at Screw U. Having studied this all-important subject during my years in that hallowed institution of higher learning, I was well equipped to write practical, yet substantive, understandings.

Virtually every sentence in my pre-typed understandings was inserted specifically to avoid a replay of some previous nightmare I had experienced during my undergraduate days at Screw U. I ultimately developed about twenty understandings, but it never ceased to amaze me how those Type Number Ones, Twos, and Threes always managed to come up with a new maneuver to try to separate me from my chips. And every time they did, I added yet another clause or two to my understandings in order to prepare for the next time I might be confronted with the same maneuver.

Because of the brevity and lack of legal terminology in my understandings, plus the fact that I had firmly established myself as someone of importance, I was usually able to get the owner to sign on the dotted line without his summoning Legalman. It was critical to get the agreement signed quickly during that first meeting while my posture was at its peak.

In this regard, two items were of particular importance. First, I extracted as much information as possible from the owner over the phone so the blanks in the agreement—with the exception of the asking price—were pretty much filled in prior to my arriving at the owner's office. Second, in the event some changes did have to be made in the agreement, they could be made quickly and easily because of my modus operandi of traveling with a fully equipped office.

I developed these two techniques specifically to avoid the possibility of having to fumble around at the moment of truth. I was cognizant of the fact that there was a point in time when the iron was as hot as it was going to get, and that it was critical to strike at that time—i.e., to get the agreement signed before things cooled down.

If the seller signed my understanding (read, *commission agreement*), I looked at it, in football terms, as the equivalent of starting out first-and-ten on my own twenty yard line, with 80 percent of the field still standing between me and the goal line.

CHAPTER 11

ADVANCING THE BALL
TO MIDFIELD

Finding a market for the properties I had under contract was the least difficult of the five selling steps, because it's to a buyer's advantage to look at as many deals as possible. And since a buyer normally has no financial obligation to an agent, he welcomes any and all submissions. He has everything to gain and nothing to lose by looking.

The catch is that most buyers are not really buyers at all. I wasted an enormous amount of time, effort, and money before I finally realized that most people who claim to be real estate buyers seldom, if ever, actually buy anything. Just as sellers are continually able to lure real estate agents into working on unmakeable deals, so, too, are agents seduced into wasting a great deal of time and effort talking to phony buyers.

I cannot imagine a more sadistic set of circumstances than a well-meaning but naive real estate agent trying to sell an unmakeable deal to a non-serious buyer. Any agent who allows himself to get into such a situation ends up feeling like a ping-pong ball, with the would-be seller and non-serious buyer being the paddles.

How do you spot a non-serious buyer? First, you have to understand that even though an individual or company is listed as a buyer in some real estate directory does not mean that he's a *serious* buyer. Second, no matter how big a real estate company may be, it doesn't necessarily mean that it is actively involved in the purchase of properties. In fact, I found that the vast majority of public companies listed in real estate directories are focused on specialty fields such as hotels and nursing homes, building their own properties, or making interim mortgage loans.

Even those who really are interested in purchasing properties are often "out of the market" at any given time. (That is to say, they are not currently purchasing properties because they either don't have enough cash available or are concentrating their efforts on problems with existing properties.) So even though the names of prospective real estate buyers are readily available to any real estate agent, it's wise to make the effort to qualify such buyers before sending them submissions.

Over a period of time, I became adept at spotting non-serious buyers, because they all tend to talk and behave in the same manner. For example, if you ask a non-serious buyer about his guidelines for purchasing properties, he will most likely tell you that he doesn't have any guidelines and that he's "willing to look at anything." But the fact is that most serious buyers *do* have definite guidelines, because they know exactly what they're looking for.

Another tip-off to a non-serious buyer is that he tends to dwell on questions of secondary importance, such as those pertaining to location, construction, and/or age of the property. As I previously pointed out, such questions are reasonable, but not until the buyer is first satisfied with the numbers and has decided that he has a definite interest in purchasing the property. If the numbers don't add up, it doesn't matter where the property is located, how well it's built, or how old it is. Serious, sophisticated buyers get down to the nuts and bolts of the numbers right away, because they understand the mathematical guidelines for evaluating cash flow—again, the *key* factor when it comes to evaluating income-producing properties.

In addition to having everything to gain and nothing to lose by looking at as many deals as possible, a non-serious buyer figures there's always a chance that he might run across a "steal"— a deal where the numbers are too good to be true. I should say, however, that if I had ever been lucky enough to work on a so-called *steal* (which, by the way, I wasn't—nor am I certain that such an animal even exists), I certainly would not have needed to call upon a non-serious buyer. I had plenty of serious buyers who would have been delighted to gobble up such a property.

In order to locate serious buyers, I used a technique similar to the one I used for finding makeable deals. My initial objectives were to learn what type of properties a buyer was interested in and what his general guidelines were for analyzing such properties. It was much easier to get buyers to come to the phone than it was to get through to owners, because, as I pointed out, it's in the buyer's best interest to work with as many real estate agents as possible.

Also, since the buyer normally has no commission obligation to the agent, he can take an ostrich attitude toward the issue of the agent's commission. Buyers usually find it all too convenient to hide their heads in the sand when the seller starts to cut off the agent's fingers at the closing. The buyer's stand pat excuse when the finger-cutting ceremony begins is: "The commission is between you (the agent) and the seller. I don't want to get involved." The compassion emanating from the buyer is enough to bring tears to one's eyes.

It would be appropriate to describe the buyer's attitude as premeditated apathy, a phenomenon you can observe all around you in just about every walk of life. If something doesn't directly affect their own well-being, most people—particularly when it comes to money—are quick to use the excuse, "I don't want to get involved." Real-life stories of people ignoring the cries of someone being murdered are well known. True, few real estate agents are murdered at closings, but commission muggings certainly are common.

My initial purpose in calling a buyer was to find out what his guidelines were so I would not waste a lot of time sending him information about properties that did not meet his criteria. This was a problem, however, because even though a buyer was more than happy to receive submissions, I knew that he would not be receptive to answering questions for a real estate agent over the phone. So, just as I had done with property owners, I took the initiative and suggested that I first send the buyer some information about myself and my operation. Into the mail went my spectacular Earth brochure, again followed by a telephone call a week later. As with sellers, the reaction among buyers was that The Tortoise must be "somebody."

When I called the buyer the second time, I was not "just another real estate agent"; I was the mysterious expert from afar who used a spectacular hardcover brochure as his calling card. During the second call, I explained that since we were both (meaning the buyer *and* me) busy people, I thought it would save a lot of time if he could answer a few quick questions over the phone. That way, I explained, I could avoid sending him properties that did not fall within his guidelines.

Already possessing a strong posture because of the image I had created from the outset, I was usually able to gain the buyer's cooperation with respect to my request. For purposes of recording the information, I developed a Buyer Information Form, which, when filled out, allowed me to make a quick determination as to whether or not a property fit a buyer's guidelines.

The first question on the form was unusual, to say the least. It asked whether the buyer was a principal or a broker. The reality was that not only were most of the entities who were listed as buyers in real estate directories not serious or currently active buyers, many of them were really just brokers posing as buyers. Who needs another broker? The difference between their modus operandi and mine was that I was actually doing the hard lifting necessary not only to locate sellers, but to get them under contract and close deals, while these fake buyers were doing nothing more than acting as passive middlemen.

As an example, a large construction company might have been listed as a real estate buyer even though it had never purchased a property. The president of that company, however, might just happen to be a licensed real estate broker who took other agents' deals (submitted to him because of his company's misleading classification as a buyer) and resubmitted them to legitimate buyers in the hopes of sharing commissions. Very cute.

Why would the big-shot head of a substantial real estate firm be interested in earning a real estate commission when he seemingly had bigger fish to fry? I found that a common, naive trait among real estate agents was their failure to understand that no matter how wealthy a principal may be, he is never above raking a few commission chips off the table for himself. One of the reasons that the rich get richer is because of the very fact they are *always* interested in acquiring more chips! In *The Art of the Deal*, Donald Trump says (in alluding to what he believed to be a $10,000 overcharge by a subcontractor) that if the time ever came when he was no longer willing to give his attention to a $10,000 charge, he'd quit the business.

Because of the shock value of my unusual first question, I found that the "buyer" would normally, in a reflexive manner, tell me the truth—or, at the very least, stutter around enough to make it obvious to me that he was, in fact, primarily interested in acting as a broker. And once I became convinced that he was just a broker fronting as a buyer, I immediately eliminated him from my list of prospective buyers.

If, however, the buyer managed to answer that all-important first question satisfactorily, I would then breeze through the rest of the form in a minute or two. The more deals I submitted to a buyer, and the more I questioned him about the deals that were not of interest to him, the more specific the information I was able to add to his form.

Most important, after a reasonable period of time I was able to tell whether he was a serious buyer or just a curiosity seeker. Curiosity seekers infiltrate every business and every walk of life, and, for the sake of efficiency, it's important to weed them out as early as possible. And to do that, you have to become adept at recognizing their wide variety of intimidating pitches and disguises.

Why would someone choose to be a curiosity seeker? Who knows? Maybe he's bored. Or insane. Or maybe it's just human nature. Whatever the reason, I strongly suggest that you not waste time trying to figure it out. Instead, learn to write off curiosity seekers as just another one of those great mysteries of life.

Ultimately, I put together a small but valuable hard-core group of serious buyers with whom I developed excellent personal relationships. It is somewhat of a paradox that even though an agent, in most cases, technically works for the seller, it is the buyer with whom he has an ongoing relationship.

Was it really in the best interest of each of my buyers to see me get paid? After all, in theory a buyer can purchase a property for a lower price if the seller does not have to pay a commission. True, but since the relationship between an agent and buyer has the potential of being long term, and since a serious buyer wants to look at as many deals as possible, it actually is in his best interest for a *productive* agent to receive his full commission at every closing.

When it comes to a buyer's determining how valuable a continuing relationship with an agent is, the deciding factor is how well the agent does his job. That's why I considered it to be so important to have a strong posture in the eyes of the buyer as well as the seller. My objective was to have each buyer consider me to be such a valuable resource that he would be motivated not to resort to premeditated apathy when it came time for my commission to be paid. The ideal, of course, would be for him to insist upon my being paid as a condition of the closing.

Unfortunately, I never quite achieved that status with most of my buyers, although the majority of them did give me their moral support (which was nice, but, to my dismay, my landlord refused to accept moral support as payment for my office rent). Even so, the buyer's moral support was valuable, because an agent who has both the buyer and seller plotting against him may as well avoid the bloodshed (i.e., his own) and not even bother to show up at the closing. In other words, better moral support than outright apathy.

Before going on to the third step of selling, I'd like to give you an example of what can happen to an agent when he doesn't have the support of the buyer. It was a situation in which I had all the legal tools on my side—a real estate license in the state where the property was located, a signed commission agreement with the owner, and heaps of certified mail—yet still managed to lose my chips. The buyer ("Charlie Cheet") was primarily a developer of large apartment projects, but he had recently put out the word that he was interested in purchasing existing apartment developments. Because I viewed Charlie as an exceptional prospect, I paid a personal visit to him at his office in Florida for the purpose of finding out what his guidelines were.

A short time after returning from Florida, I sent Charlie, by certified mail, a presentation on a group of apartment properties in Houston, the asking price for which was $10 million. Then, a curious thing happened. From out of the blue, I received a call from a total stranger ("Larry Lyar") who told me that he was "associated with" Charlie Cheet. I was not yet sophisticated enough to understand that vague expressions such as "associated with" are almost always an early warning sign that a commission heist is on the horizon. Larry emphasized that he did not work for Charlie as an employee, but as an independent "associate" (another red-flag word that often translates into "unemployed flake") who had the responsibility of reviewing deals for him. He said that, in return, Charlie gave him a participation in any properties acquired through him.

Perhaps by this time I was a bit overconfident and didn't realize that no matter how much experience a broker had, there was always another vile creature lurking in the depths of the Jungle who was capable of coming up with yet another new gimmick. There is, however, a common thread that runs through every new gimmick, no matter how clever or well-concealed it may be: It's always designed to separate you from your chips!

As always, I did a first-class job gathering all the data on the properties and putting together a professional presentation. However, I did not present the information to Charlie Cheet, the apartment-builder-turned-buyer, but to his "associate," Larry Lyar. (This now-puzzling decision gave me the distinction of demonstrating that I could do a perfect imitation of Homer Simpson years before he was even created.) I even went to the expense of flying Larry to Houston to inspect the properties, and spent a great deal of time wining and dining him.

Following our trip, every time I asked Larry what the status of the deal was, he assured me that he and Charlie Cheet were "working on the numbers" and would soon give me an answer. This went on for months, until I finally assumed that Charlie Cheet was not a serious buyer.

That mistake led to the birth of the Assumption Theory, which states: *Assume nothing! If your mother says she loves you, check it out.*

I woke up one day to find that my assumption had been entirely wrong. Charlie not only was a serious buyer, he had already closed the Houston deal without my knowledge! Larry Lyar, of course, was nothing more than a blue-suede-shoe broker who got a commission out of the deal without even having to split it with the reptile who had presented it to him and who had done all the work. Shame on me. I had gotten caught in a classic chip-pilfering sting. As you might have guessed, I'm not real close with Charlie Cheet and Larry Lyar anymore.

Why did I not sue Charlie Cheet when I had all three legal tools in my possession? Because by this time I had a pretty good understanding of *practical law* (as opposed to theoretical law). Consider the following:

1. Both Charlie Cheet and the seller claimed that they had been talking to each other about the properties before I had registered Charlie with the seller. (At no time during our negotiations had either of them even hinted at such a thing, let alone made an issue of it. By contrast, my treacherous Type Number Two professor in the Missouri Massacre had at least had the decency to let me know early on that, notwithstanding the indisputable facts, he intended to stick it to me and not give me credit for the buyer I had brought to him.) So not only was the buyer not giving me his moral support, he was actually siding with the seller. Any time that the buyer and seller are willing to lie in concert, it's time to fold 'em— time to extract the lesson learned and go take a disinfectant bubble bath.

2. Charlie Cheet refused to accept any responsibility for Larry Lyar's actions, insisting that he had never authorized Larry to say that he was his associate or in any way represented him. Though Charlie sugar-coated his words, his position, plain and simple, was that it was my tough luck if I had been taken in by a serial liar. (Is all this starting to sound similar to some memorable experience out of your own past?)

3. Larry Lyar, upstanding young lad that he was, in turn insisted that I had somehow misunderstood him and that he had never told me he was associated with the buyer. In Jungle terms, this one fell into a category known as "The Big Lie." No matter how sophisticated or experienced you may be, it's impossible to ever be fully prepared to cope with a Jungle creature who is willing to up the stakes by telling The Big Lie. Regardless of

what legal tools you may have on your side, never forget Business World Jungle Rule No. 1: *If you insist on sleeping with big dogs, you're guaranteed to end up with big fleas.* The fleas I got from Larry were big enough to eat my wallet.

4. Even though it was obvious to me that this Jungle trio (i.e., including the seller) had succeeded in putting Ringer through the wringer, I was realistic enough to see that there was enough confusion surrounding the facts (such as the involvement of Charlie's Cheet's "associate," Larry Lyar, and Charlie's willingness to side with the seller) to give some smart litigation attorney sufficient ammunition to cloud the issue for a judge or jury.

5. Our court system is an important weapon that Jungle creatures use to offset Tortoise-like legal tools. Because of the time involved in bringing a case such as this to trial, the guy in the wrong almost always has the advantage. After some cursory investigation, I concluded that it would take anywhere from three to five years for the matter to be resolved in court, and, in the meantime, I would not only have to come up with bushels of cash to pay onerous legal fees and court costs, I also would have to invest considerable time and energy and be further aggravated in the process.

6. There was a strong rumor that the seller of the properties might have to declare bankruptcy (apparently the proceeds of the sale were not enough to bail him out of his troubles), and, after investigating the rumor, I concluded that his imminent financial demise was a definite possibility. This being the case, I recognized that even if I won in court, it could prove to be a chipless victory.

When I weighed all the facts, it simply did not add up to a smart gamble of my time, energy, and money to pursue the matter. I had already learned that the Jungle has its own set of rules for meting out justice—something about survival of the fittest, or some such thing. Plain and simple, if you lose your case in the Jungle, you lose your case—*period*.

My lesson in the Houston deal again confirmed that even though the buyer does not normally pay the broker's commission, it was important to develop good relationships with my buyers. Had the buyer of the Houston deal been on my side, it could have made a major difference in the outcome.

Notwithstanding the Houston fiasco, once I had obtained a product to sell and had at least one serious buyer whose Buyer Information Form indicated that he was a good prospect for the kind of property I was offering, I considered myself to have accomplished sales step number two: locating a market for my product.

In metaphorical football terms, I had advanced the ball to perhaps midfield—which meant I still had a long way to go to reach the end zone.

CHAPTER 12

REACHING THE OPPONENT'S
TWENTY YARD LINE

Again, it was of prime importance to me to perform at a high level, not only because it gave me credibility with both buyers and sellers, but should I ever have to take legal action to collect a commission, I felt my performance would be a major factor in my favor.

I worked out a system for gathering property information and preparing presentations that not only was incredibly detailed, but unique in concept. My information-gathering system made it possible for a person with very little real estate knowledge to obtain the pertinent facts quickly. Just as I had managed, through experience, to develop commission agreements that became increasingly sophisticated, I likewise developed a series of "Property Data Forms" to fit every conceivable type of situation.

126

I taught several of my secretaries how to use these forms quickly and efficiently, which made it possible for me to make my exit after obtaining a signed commission agreement from the owner of a property. Leaving one of my secretaries behind to gather the property information was a big step forward, because it freed me to work on other deals. After my secretary had gathered all the information, she would return to my office and submit her completed form to another person who would then use her material to prepare a professional presentation of the property. When the presentation was completed, I would review my Buyer Information Forms (discussed in the previous chapter) and decide who were the best prospects were for that particular property.

I would then implement my third legal tool: certified mail. Certified mail was a potential savior, because in the event I should have to take legal action to collect a commission, certified-mail slips could be the deciding factor. It was a good example of recognizing and acknowledging reality—the reality that I might have to take legal action to collect a commission, no matter how hard I tried to avoid becoming embroiled in a lawsuit. If I never needed to use the certified-mail slips, all the better, but a certified-mail slip is like a gun: When you need it, you need it bad and you need it fast. Hence, I made it an ironclad rule to send every presentation by certified mail. You may think I was a bit paranoid, but future events proved that no matter to what extremes I went to protect myself in the Jungle, I was, in fact, almost always *under*protected.

About a week after I sent a presentation by certified mail, I would call the prospective buyer to see if he had an interest in further discussing the property. If he was not interested, I would try to find out precisely why, then note the reason or reasons on his Buyer Information Form. But if he indicated that he did have an interest in the property, I would immediately register his name with the owner via my new best friend—certified mail.

My next objective was to get the prospective buyer to meet with the seller and inspect his property. To bring this about,

I focused on getting as much relevant information as possible flowing back and forth between the buyer and seller. Given that my primary objective was to make certain I received my full commission if the deal were to close, a steady flow of information moving between buyer and seller was of no small importance. Why? Because, among other things, it would be clear evidence that I was the major force not only in bringing the buyer and seller together, but in getting the deal closed. Sellers *hate* paying a commission to a real estate agent who does nothing more than introduce him to a buyer.

Regardless of what business you're in, when it comes to sales or deal-making, it's critical that you to build a detailed record of your involvement—not just to use as a last resort in court, but as a constant reminder to all the principals involved that you are/ were instrumental in making the deal happen.

Because of my strong posture, I was normally able to keep the lines of communication flowing *through* me rather than *around* me—a psychological necessity when it comes to maintaining one's posture. Long-distance telephone calls were also important, because they became a matter of record and, if necessary, could help to substantiate the degree of my involvement in a deal. Never forget that your landline and cell phone bills are permanent, irrefutable records that have the power to destroy that most devastating of all Jungle weapons—The Big Lie.

If a buyer told me that he would like to speak directly with the seller, or vice versa, I handled it smoothly. Rather than displaying nervousness over such a request, which would have denoted weakness, without hesitation I indicated that I thought it was an excellent idea (even though I really thought it was a horrible idea). However, I subtly maintained control of the situation by *telling* (rather than asking) the buyer or seller, whichever the case may have been, that *I* would set up a conference call among the *three* of us. The key here was that I neither hesitated nor asked anyone's permission. Rather, I responded immediately and stated, with confidence and authority, precisely how the request would be handled. As a bonus, being bold and taking the initiative added to my already strong posture.

I knew all too well that if I allowed the buyer and seller to talk to each other without my being on the phone, I would be asking for my first posture puncture. Posture maintenance is a delicate matter. No matter how slight that first puncture may be, its nature is to spread. For this reason, I always tactfully and subtly tried to block any direct conversation between the buyer and seller, because I knew that private communication between two carnivores could be the first step toward shutting me out.

There was only one thing more dangerous than the buyer and seller talking to each by phone, and that was (Gasp!) their meeting face-to-face without my being present. Of course, I didn't need to worry about that possibility until I had the buyer interested enough in the property to be willing to spend the time and money to travel to the seller's city.

My feeling about getting the buyer to inspect the property was very much like that of a life insurance salesman who feels that he's three-quarters of the way toward making a sale if he can just persuade the prospective client to take a physical examination. If a buyer was motivated enough to fly to a distant city to meet the seller and inspect his property, I then metaphorically thought of myself as being in scoring position. Obviously, no sale was going to take place until the buyer made such a trip. Sure, he could determine his initial interest based on a handful of figures he had received up to that point, but there was no way he was going to get serious about a purchase until he had personally met the seller and stared at a few bricks.

In this regard, I did two things to expedite the prospective buyer's decision to get on an airplane. First, I spoon-fed him any and all information he requested. It was important to take matters into my own hands and remove as much responsibility as possible from the other parties involved. If, for example, there were legal questions about the mortgage, instead of spending several days trying to track down the seller's attorney, then waiting several more days for him to get back to me with an answer, I would undertake to research the needed information myself.

I actually trained one of my secretaries to read mortgages, mortgage notes, deeds of trust, mortgage-commitment letters, and most other documents involved in real estate closings. She got so good at it that she often was able to obtain the answer to a buyer's legal question in fifteen minutes or so, which made it possible to avoid waiting a week or two to get the answer from some lazy, negligent, fee-building attorney. Of course, some lawyers might protest that she was violating the government-enforced legal monopoly laws regarding the practice of law, but from my standpoint she was merely saving everyone time and money by finding the information the buyer had requested. And, to boot, she wasn't arrogant about it, she returned phone calls promptly, she conveyed the information in an intelligible manner, and she didn't bill at the rate of $300 an hour. Nirvana for an entrepreneur.

Similarly, if an accounting question came up, I found that by taking matters into my own hands by having one of my people work on it, I could usually come up with the answer in a matter of minutes, whereas it might have taken a week or two to track down the seller's accountant to obtain an answer.

The second thing I did in an effort to hasten the buyer's decision to visit the owner's property was to continually impress upon him my belief that all his questions could be answered quickly if he would meet with the seller and personally inspect his property. Each time I obtained another answer for him, I reemphasized the point that a trip was sure to save him a lot of time in the long run. If the buyer was really serious, my gentle, repeated suggestion would usually result in a commitment to make the trip. Experience had taught me that it was critical to get the buyer to personally inspect the property at the earliest possible date, because time is always against the person who is trying hardest to get the deal closed.

That's because time brings into play the Fiddle Theory, which states: *The longer you fiddle around with a deal, the greater the odds that it will never close.*

Nero fiddled while Rome burned, and too many salesmen and entrepreneurs do likewise as they watch their deals go up in smoke. This reality is as true in any other aspect of life as it is in a business deal. Never forget that time is your enemy when it comes to closing deals. Why? Because circumstances constantly change! In a real estate deal, for example, the mortgage lender may suddenly decide that it wants an unreasonable fee in exchange for allowing the property to be transferred to another owner, the seller's wife may talk him out of going through with the sale, or the buyer may close another deal and decide that he doesn't want to make any more purchases for a while.

The only thing I could be certain would never change was my desire to collect a commission, so I had a big incentive to keep pushing everything forward as quickly as possible. Consequently, I tried to undertake as much responsibility as I could and avoid relying on the seller's motivation to sell or the buyer's motivation to buy. The only motivation I could count on to remain constant was *my* motivation to collect a commission.

The Fiddle Theory and the Tortoise and Hare Theory fit together like the proverbial hand and glove. As The Tortoise, I had always trudged ahead relentlessly, hoping that the other guy would momentarily relax. By not fiddling around, I always figured that I might get there a week, a day, an hour, or even a minute earlier, which experience had taught me could mean the difference between making or losing a sale. The experience I had in Tampa years earlier—showing up at the bank first thing in the morning and collecting my $15,000 commission in cash—was always at the forefront of my mind and kept me focused on the importance of the Fiddle Theory.

By assuming as much responsibility as possible for answering questions and gathering information, and by continually suggesting to the buyer that he could probably have all his questions answered at one time if he would personally visit the owner, I often was able to speed up the buyer's decision to inspect the property. This was of great importance, because once he made the decision to invest in a trip, I knew I was getting close to scoring territory.

Whenever possible, I would make arrangements to travel to the *buyer's* city ahead of time so he and I could "review the details of the deal on the plane" on the way to seller's city. In reality, of course, I had ulterior motives for making such an out-of-the-way trip. First, I wanted to make certain that the buyer and seller did not meet before I arrived. Second, it gave me the opportunity to develop a more personal relationship with the buyer and hopefully inspire in him a sense of loyalty to me.

At best, I was hoping to make my relationship with the buyer so tight that he would refuse to go through with a closing if the seller started to reach for my chips. At a minimum, I wanted to nurture our relationship to the point where the buyer would at least feel uncomfortable being a party to a closing in which a game of pin-the-tail-on-the-tortoise was an entertaining side attraction.

If I was unable to accompany the prospective buyer on his flight to the city where the property was located, I did the next best thing: I met his plane at the gate when it landed. One way or another, I wanted to make certain that I was always positioned between the buyer and seller, which is why I took the initiative in all aspects of the negotiations.

In previous years, my knowledge had usually been more than sufficient, but because of my weak posture, it hadn't resulted in big paydays. Now my posture was strong, because I possessed both image power and legal power. My objective at these buyer-seller meetings was to display so much knowledge about the property and the closing of the deal that even the seller would be embarrassed to challenge my right to a commission. (If you're chuckling and shaking your head from side to side over that last comment, you're starting to get it, because my objective proved to be nothing more than wishful thinking. Sellers *always* challenge agents' commissions.)

From start to finish I did everything within my power to see to it that the buyer and seller were never together without my being present. You might say that The Tortoise portrayed Mary's Little Lamb—everywhere the buyer went, I was sure to go. When all the buyer's questions had been answered and a deal had been structured, I personally accompanied him to the airport. I never left town first, even if it meant missing my last flight out and having to stay overnight. Not until the buyer's plane had pulled safely away from the gate did I shed my lambskin and revert back to being a tortoise.

If everything went as planned, and the buyer and seller verbally committed to moving forward with a deal, I had successfully accomplished sales step number three: implementation of a marketing strategy. At that point I considered myself to be in scoring position—at about the opponent's twenty yard line. I knew I was getting close, because I could see the blood of all those long-forgotten intimidatees who had dared to try to score in previous games.

As most everyone knows, however, moving the ball those last twenty yards is a real gut check. It's where the defense gets nasty and the play gets ugly. No doubt about it, a tortoise has to be prepared to leave it all on the field in order to cross the goal line.

"I could swear you look different than when I saw you in New York, but I can't seem to put my finger on what it is."

CHAPTER 13

SCORING

Invariably, shortly after the buyer and seller arrived at a general agreement on the terms of a sale, a strange thing would occur: would-be purchasers suddenly started beating a path to the seller's door. It was like magic. For months, even years, the seller had not been able to find a serious buyer for his property prior to my entering the picture. Then, suddenly, it seemed as though people were standing in line to buy his project after we had already verbally agreed to the terms of a deal.

This phenomenon occurred with such regularity that I eventually came to anticipate it in every deal. And once I recognized it as a pattern, I figured out a way to use it to my benefit. I took on the aura of a clairvoyant by assuring the seller, well in advance, that once I found a serious buyer for him, "wannabe buyers" would start banging on his door. I cautioned the seller not to take such Johnny-come-lately offers seriously, because if such "buyers" had a legitimate interest in his property, they would have stepped up to the plate a long time ago. Consequently, when phantom offers began to make their predictable appearance, it served only to add to my already strong posture, because it reaffirmed in the buyer's mind that I knew what I was talking about.

It's important to analyze what caused this sudden barrage of phony offers to appear each time I was about to close a sale, because, once again, the psychology behind it affects every area of one's life.

It's a phenomenon that can be explained by the Boy-Girl Theory, which states: *Everyone wants what he can't have, and does not want what he can have.*

It doesn't get any more basic than this. The Boy-Girl Theory is one of the most basic human instincts. I would guess it was around even in the days of Cro-Magnon Man. There are very few adults, if any, who have not played the boy-girl game in high school, college, or beyond. In high school, the easiest way for a guy to land a girl (or vice versa) is to "play it cool." In contrast, he can virtually assure that he will *not* land the object of his affection if he salivates on his shirt every time she walks by.

Unfortunately, this motivating force doesn't stop in high school or college; it stops when life ends on Planet Earth. When you see a guy who looks like a compressed version of Frankenstein's Monster walking down the street with a gorgeous woman on his arm, you can't help but wonder what she could possibly see in him. What you are probably witnessing is the result of the Boy-Girl Theory—physical shortcomings notwithstanding, the mini-monster probably is a master at playing it cool. Women love men who play hard to get; men love women who play hard to get. And we accuse animals of acting on instinct?

Beware: The same psychology applies in business. No matter how successful a person may be, human nature is such that he is inclined to want the deal he *can't* have and not want the

"Oooh, Frankie, you're such a brute."

deal he *can* have. Because of this reality, the nearer one of my deals got to a closing, the more other buyers, both serious and non-serious, imagined they wanted to buy the property because, much like the gal who's about to get married, it would soon be unavailable. The apartment development that had been on the market for months or years was about to become a bride!

In most cases, of course, this sudden surge of offers amounted to nothing more than a panic reaction on the part of fellow real estate agents and buyers. Since other agents had absolutely nothing to lose by inundating an owner with *verbal* offers, I could usually count on a herd of these characters crawling out from under their rocks as a closing began to look more like a probability than a possibility. It cost them absolutely nothing to make verbal offers that sounded more attractive than mine, but coming up with cash was quite another matter.

Once the Boy-Girl Theory took effect, invariably it would lead to a corollary phenomenon: Not only did other buyers suddenly start imagining that they wanted the property, but often the seller would begin thinking that he did *not* want my buyer's offer, because it was a deal that was now in hand. Psychologically speaking, once he had a written offer, it became the woman who was too available.

I call this second phenomenon the Better-Deal Theory, which states: *Before a person closes a deal, it's human nature for him to worry that there may be a better deal down the road.*

This is a theory that holds true regardless of whether the deal involves real estate, insurance, vacuum sweepers, the acquisition of a billion-dollar company—or a potential spouse. It's an almost uncontrollable urge for a person to wonder, at the last moment, if he might not be missing out on a better deal somewhere down the road.

Because of this instinct, the seller's mind was open to the last-minute verbal offers that were sure to be directed at him. He was ripe for the phony buyers who came prancing in at the eleventh hour, because the thought had already crossed his mind that if he closed the deal I had secured for him, he might miss out on an opportunity for a better price on his property just around the next bend. So when real estate agents came scurrying to him with offers from mysterious clients at the last moment, he *wanted* to believe their offers were real. Greed is a great catalyst for causing one's wishes to override reality. As a result, the seller would be much more inclined to take seriously an offer that, under normal circumstances, he probably would have quickly dismissed as having no substance.

To combat the negative effects of the Boy-Girl Theory and the Better Deal Theory, my objective was to do everything within my power to bring the deal as quickly as possible to the point where the money was on the table and the papers were ready to be signed. Then it was put-up-or-shut-up time—time for the army of mysterious buyers to put up their money or crawl back under their rocks. I'm happy to report that rarely did they do any putting up, and usually it was just a matter of time until the seller would begin to question whether there really was a better deal down the road.

Once my buyer's chips were on the table, the Boy-Girl Theory would begin to have a reverse effect in my favor, because a serious buyer does not leave his cash lying around forever. The more a seller hesitated, the more likely the buyer would begin to show signs of having second thoughts himself about the closing. And when that happened, it tended to cause the seller to better appreciate the bird in the hand—the deal he might lose if he didn't get on the stick and get it closed. The fact that real estate agents and phony buyers hated to see the property being taken out of circulation didn't matter to the seller once he realized that they were unable or unwilling to come up with cash when my buyer's chips were already on the table.

To bring the deal to the put-up-or-shut-up stage as quickly as possible, I always tried to analyze what the real objectives of the buyer and seller were, as well as what their key objections were. I say *analyze* rather than *find out*, because it has been my experience that parties to a deal very often are not consciously aware of what their real objectives and objections are. Also, because of a variety of ulterior motives—or out of pure embarrassment—either the buyer or seller, or both, might purposely suppress their true objectives and/or objections.

Two objectives of which I could always be certain, however, were that the buyer wanted to buy the property for the lowest possible price and the seller wanted to sell the property for the highest possible price—the epitome of a conflict of interest. This is precisely what selling is all about. If there were no basic conflict of interest between the buyer's and seller's objectives, there would be no need for an agent. The better an agent is at being able to resolve this inherent conflict of interest, the better his chances of earning (though not necessarily receiving) his commission.

If I was able to correctly analyze and satisfy the basic objectives and objections of the buyer and seller—especially the basic conflict over price —I then focused on the shortest route to a closing: Taking it upon myself to assume as much responsibility as possible. The Fiddle Theory was always foremost in my mind, because once the buyer and seller spelled out the terms of a deal, I knew that time was of the essence. An extra week, extra day, or even extra hour might mean the difference between making or breaking the sale.

Just as I had done in implementing my techniques for finding deals, I tried not to depend on the performance of any of the other parties. From the moment the buyer and seller verbally agreed to the terms of a sale, my entire office staff was available twenty-four hours a day. There was no way I was going to allow my commission to be tied to the abilities and/or motivation of the buyer or seller to get things done, nor to the incompetence, apathy, and/or negligence of their secretaries, attorneys, or accountants.

I recognized early on that documents were a key element in getting a deal closed. In fact, I considered some documents to be so important that, if a big enough commission was at stake, I would not hesitate to have one of my secretaries fly to a city to pick them up from one of the parties, then fly to another city to hand-deliver them to the appropriate party. Once I was inside the twenty yard line, the stakes were big enough, and the odds in favor of a closing high enough, to make it worthwhile to risk a significant amount of time and capital in an effort to ward off unnecessary delays.

My techniques often astonished the employees of both the buyer and seller. Life, for them, was quite simple. If someone requested some information from them, they gathered it at their leisure, put it in an envelope, applied a first-class postage stamp, and dropped it in a mail box at the end of the day. To pick up the telephone and call the information in to the party requesting it, which might save three or four days, was unthinkable. And to board an airplane and hand-carry a document to someone was total insanity. Only a tortoise would be crazy enough to do such a thing—and I often did. (Little did I know that a technology called "e-mail" would soon descend upon the Milky Way Galaxy, which would usually alleviate the need to resort to such rash action.)

Plain and simple, if you aspire to a high success rate when it comes to getting results, you must shake the habit of assuming that someone—particularly someone whom you do not know very well—will see to it that important details are taken care of. Instead, get in the habit of taking matters into your own hands and moving swiftly once the goal line is in sight. Think of yourself as a great quarterback: When the game gets down to those final minutes, take control of things yourself!

If all went well, I succeeded in advancing the ball to the one yard line, the point at which the chips were on the table and the documents ready to be signed. But that last yard is almost always the most brutal to gain. My education at Screw U. had taught me that when I arrived in town for the long-awaited closing, there were still two potential obstacles that could keep me from scoring.

The first and most awesome obstacle was the Attorney Goal Line Defense. No NFL team can match the Attorney Goal Line

Defense in intensity. Simply put, there is no way that any attorney worth his salt is going to just sit back and allow a deal to close without at least putting up a fight.

There we were—the buyer, the seller, and me—sitting in a room together, chips on the table, the deal ready to close. Predictably, at that point, who should appear on the scene? Not Superman ... not Plasticman ... not Cookieman. Lo and behold, it was none other than—alert the media—*Legalman!* Onto the field he would trot, flapping his Brooks Brothers cape in the wind and cackling as he opened his briefcase full of little deal-killing goodies. "Would this be an easy one to kill?" he wondered to himself. Would he be able to destroy this deal without working up a sweat, or would this be one of those rare but difficult challenges for him?

Legalman would immediately begin to implement the "he-we-I" evolution strategy. At the outset, he would talk in terms of *he* (the seller) in discussing the property and the closing. Then, in a relatively short period of time, the word *he* would subtly evolve into *we* (i.e., the seller *and* Legalman). At that point, the seller was no longer in full control of his destiny. Nay, it was now he *and* Legalman who were making the decisions. Finally—you guessed it—Legalman, in a galling display of arrogance, would magically transform *we* into *I* (as in *Legalman*). Some things in life are inevitable, and Legalman's "he-we-I" evolution strategy is one of those inevitabilities. From that point on, it was entirely Legalman's deal. The buyer and seller had been reduced to nothing more than bothersome but necessary bystanders to *Legalman's* closing.

Of course, if the buyer and seller were nothing more than necessary but bothersome bystanders in the eyes of Legalman, you can just imagine how he viewed The Tortoise. He might have considered me to be bothersome, but he certainly could see no reason why I was necessary. As a result, when Legalman made his initial entrance into the deal, he was usually taken aback by my strong posture. After all, wasn't I "just a real estate broker?" What was I even doing at the closing, anyway? How dare I not be intimidated?

*"I haven't given up a score in the last eight deals,
and I don't intend to start now."*

In order to understand how incredible such a situation was for Legalman to digest, you have to appreciate the fact that there are many natural predators in the Jungle, creatures whose survival depends upon the killing of their prey. One of those predators is Legalman, and he preys upon deals. (I'm not sure whether that makes him a carnivore or herbivore.) The fact is that Legalman's financial survival depends upon his ability to kill deals, and the creatures who spawn those deals are more often than not salesmen, businessmen, and entrepreneurs. Where Legalman is concerned, we're talking about a literal life-or-death matter here. After all, if every deal closed smoothly, he could become an endangered species.

Talk about a conflict of interest. My singular focus was to get the ball over the goal line, while Legalman's training had specifically prepared him to keep green upstarts like me from moving the ball that last yard. Anyone who cannot fully grasp the reality that the primary function of Legalman is to kill deals would be wise to keep his job at Walmart and not step foot inside the Business World Jungle.

Honesty compels me to add that I do not blame Legalman for his deal-killing ways, given that his law-school training specifically prepared him for the life of a predator. A Phi Beta Kappa friend of mind once told me that during his three years of law school, the emphasis was almost entirely on how to *find* problems. He said he could not remember a single course that was focused on how to solve problems. With that kind of training, why *shouldn't* we expect Legalman to be a deal assassin? Bringing him into a deal is like throwing him a piece of raw meat. (Hmmm ... maybe he is a carnivore.)

I figured out early on that Legalman would expect me to come crashing through the middle of the line to try to pick up that last yard, and that he would set his defenses accordingly. So, to cross him up, I would usually try to finesse my way over the goal line. With a well-executed end sweep, or perhaps a screen pass to the outside, I might just be able to make that last yard untouched. Straight up the middle would be asking for a bloody collision.

In other words, I never tried to push Legalman or get tough with him. The big fella with the cape is hard to intimidate, because his law school training continually reinforced in his brain the notion that no one merits a higher station in life than lawyers. By the same token, I realized that it would be a fatal mistake for me to cower. If there was one thing I had to give Legalman credit for, it was his killer instinct. I knew that once he sensed weakness on my part, he would ride roughshod over me. If I adopted the awed attitude that so many of my comrades in the pack had been intimidated into doing when dealing with attorneys, I knew that Legalman would knock the ball from my grasp and most likely recover the fumble.

I therefore displayed a calm, matter-of-fact attitude when in Legalman's presence. When I spoke, it was with an air that implied I had no concerns about anything, and that a closing was a foregone conclusion. Problems did not represent obstacles to a closing, but merely minor points that had to be "handled" as a natural part of every deal. Such an attitude was confusing to Legalman, because he expected me to display the typical real estate agent's panic demeanor. By acting unconcerned about each deal-killing goody that he pulled from his bag, I was able to throw Legalman off balance and thereby weaken his defenses. He was totally unprepared to deal with someone who seemed to not even acknowledge his deal-killing skills.

As Legalman injected one problem after another into a deal, I would say things like, "That's a very good point (*not* problem). I'm glad you brought it up." I would then proceed to state (*not* ask) a number of ways that we (*not* just Legalman) would (*not* could) handle (*not* solve) that particular point (again, *not* problem). But never did I directly challenge Legalman. My attitude was that it was assumed by everyone involved that there was going to be a closing, and that the only purpose of our all being present was to work together to "handle" the normal "points" that are inherent in every closing. Just business as usual.

Legalman had never been up against a tortoise before. Old standby "problems" such as needing some obscure document from the mortgage lender—problems that Legalman had always counted on to stall a closing for at least a week or two in order to give the Fiddle Theory time to take effect—were dissolved before his very eyes. I accomplished this by merely dispatching one of my secretaries cross country to pick up the document in question and hand-carry it to the party who requested it.

After handling some of Legalman's best shots in this manner, he might, if I were lucky, begin to tire and conclude that the long lunches, golf games, and martini hours he was missing by trying to keep this strange reptile from traveling one lousy yard were not worth the effort. Hopefully, then, he would ease up just enough to allow me to nudge the nose of the ball over the goal line. In other words, it was a war of attrition.

However, in the event Legalman held his ground, I implemented the Boy-Girl Theory as a last resort. In the most casual manner, I would say something to the effect of, "Well, I guess that's it. It looks as though we just won't be able to close this one." When it got to that point, it was time for the seller to fold his hand or become a big boy. Meaning it was time for him to regain control of *his* deal, time to stand up and let Legalman now that *he* was once again calling the shots.

Unfortunately, not many sellers have the nerve to take such bold action. About the only thing that seemed to work was to raise the seller's fear of losing the deal that was on the table. So if there was no other way to handle the Attorney Goal Line Defense, there was still hope if I could instill fear in the seller's heart that he was about to miss out on an opportunity to sell his property. With the psychology of the Boy-Girl Theory thrashing about in his nimble brain, he might just be willing to commit heresy and find the nerve to stand up to Legalman.

Before leaving the subject of the Attorney Goal Line Defense, I should point out that there is one factor that is even more important than all the techniques I have described for overcoming Legalman's bag of little deal-killing goodies. The factor I am referring to is financial desperation on the part of the seller. Unfortunately, a real estate agent has no direct control over this factor, but the more desperate the seller, the better the chances that he will not allow Legalman to sabotage the closing.

Even though an agent has no *direct* control over this factor, he does, of course, have indirect control by virtue of his having the power to choose which deals he works on. Which gets back to the strategy of working hard to find makeable deals rather than working on a lot of unmakeable deals in the hopes that one will accidentally close. In reality, the degree of financial desperation on the part of the seller is *the single most important factor* in determining how makeable a deal is. The more financial problems the seller has, the more success you'll have in keeping Legalman off the playing field.

In summation, it's important to grasp the reality that Legalman has been, is, and always will be a major obstacle—and, more often than not, *the* major obstacle—to closing deals. Since the general population will never understand that an attorney is nothing more than a college graduate with a fancy certificate on his wall that grants him a monopolistic right to practice intimidation on civilians, you're at a decided advantage if you are among the minority of players who possess such an understanding. Further, it is essential for you to develop techniques for protecting your deals from the clutches of this deal-thirsty predator if you aspire to achieve a high level of success in the Jungle.

Surprisingly, the buyer's attorney (as opposed to the seller's attorney) seldom caused me problems, because his client was in the business of buying properties. If the buyer was a serious professional whose main line of business was the purchase of income-producing properties, his attorney knew all too well that it was in his best interest to leave his bag of deal-killing goodies at home and do everything possible to help his client get deals closed.

The other obstacle that usually confronted me at the one-yard line was the seller's dirty laundry, which could include any one of a number of surprises. Some of the more common of these surprises were undisclosed, major liens against the property (even though the seller had repeatedly assured the buyer that none existed), the mortgage holder's refusal to allow the property to be transferred from the seller to the buyer (even though the seller had assured the buyer that the mortgagee had already given its approval for the transfer), and many more vacancies than the seller's official "rent roll" had indicated. (To this day, a favorite trick of sellers is to fill vacant apartments with relatives, friends, and employees until after a closing takes place.)

Sooner or later, a real estate agent needs to come to grips with the reality that no matter how many times the seller assures him that all the information he has submitted is correct—that there are no hidden surprises—there *will* be several major, undisclosed items of a deal-killing magnitude that surface as a sale nears the closing stage.

I always tried to soften the blow of the inevitable dirty laundry by preparing the buyer for it ahead of time. Just as I fore-warned the seller that there would be a sudden surge of phony offers once he had a verbal agreement with my buyer, so, too, did I warn the buyer that he could count on many negative surprises as we neared the closing. This not only helped to mentally prepare the buyer for the seller's inevitable dirty laundry, but again made me appear to be very savvy when the inevitable problems did arise.

Of course, I used the same kind of semantics I did when turning Legalman's problems into normal "points" that had to be "handled" as a part of every closing. I created an atmosphere of expectancy rather than surprise with regard to the inevitable appearance of the seller's dirty laundry. In addition, I found that most sophisticated buyers had enough experience to realize that a seller's closing surprises are simply part of the game. My objective was to just try to eliminate as much of the shock value of the dirty laundry as possible.

If the problems could be resolved by sending someone to another city to pick up a document or administer some persuasion, I again took matters into my own hands and did whatever had to be done. However, if the problem could not be resolved by physical means, there was always the hope that I could persuade the seller to lower his selling price enough to adjust for the dirty laundry that appeared on the scene at the last moment.

If that didn't work, I tried to see if either a sale-leaseback or contingent-payment sale could satisfy both sides. All else failing, my last resort was to again fall back on the psychology of the Boy-Girl Theory. I would talk to the buyer in private and remind him of all the reasons why it was a good deal, hoping to create a sense of fear over the possibility that he might lose the "girl."

Of course, if the dirty laundry was too outrageous—as was often the case—at some point I had to be willing to walk away from the deal. As I pointed out in the Theory of Next, there are often factors that are beyond the real estate agent's control. As a result, no matter how well I managed to finesse my way past Legalman, the seller's dirty laundry would often stop me before I crossed the goal line.

But even if I managed to get past both Legalman and the seller's dirty laundry, I still had to complete the fifth and final step of selling: *getting paid.*

After all the time, energy, and money I had spent in obtaining the product, locating a buyer, implementing a marketing method, and closing the sale, it was all for naught if I didn't get credit for the score. If I was careless enough to commit an infraction on the touchdown play, all the effort I had expended to move the ball downfield was meaningless, because closing a deal and not getting paid is analogous to scoring the winning touchdown and having it called back because of a penalty.

Above all, then, I had to become an expert at avoiding a "penalty" once I got into scoring position, and I realized that my ability to do so very much depended on my ability to defend myself against the intimidators who were ready to pounce on me the moment I tried to touch the ball.

CHAPTER 14

IT DOESN'T COUNT UNTIL THE POINTS
ARE ON THE SCOREBOARD

In successfully accomplishing the first four steps of selling, most of my efforts were directly or indirectly geared toward succeeding at the fifth and most important step: *getting paid*. Contrary to what most people naively assume, the object of the game is not to close deals. The object is to walk away with chips in your hand.

In real estate brokerage, selling a property is only a means to an end, that end being the pocketing of a commission by the real estate agent. As I have repeatedly stated, there's a big difference between *earning* a commission and *receiving* a commission. When I closed a sale, I was fully aware that I had only earned—*not* received—a commission. And to make certain that I never lost sight of what my real objective was, I carried a second card in my wallet that contained yet another literary masterpiece, to wit:

Closing deals is so much trash,
If you, my friend, don't get no cash.

Again, no Nobel Prize. Maybe someday.

In some of the most trendy success and how-to books, there is usually a great deal of emphasis placed on doing what's in the client's best interest, and I totally concur with the idea of going the extra mile for your clients. Above all, I believe in the concept of value-for-value. Nonetheless, it's curious to me that no book ever seems to address what's in the best interest of the salesman, broker, finder, or other person who puts the deal together—in real estate or in any other field. Above all, I have never seen anything written in any success or sales book about how to accomplish the most important step of selling: *getting paid.*

At Screw U. I had come to the conclusion that the emphasis of most salesmen, entrepreneurs, and deal-makers is misdirected. It is, indeed, noble to have the client's best interest at heart, but your wife and kids might feel just a bit more secure if you also had *your* (and their) best interest at heart as well. I never walked away from a closing without feeling that I had performed a valuable service for my client, so I had no trouble sleeping at night on that score. What was a problem, however, was that the principals in most of my deals seemed to consider me to be out of line if I dared to suggest that I'd like to get paid for my services. Liberal fantasies aside, in case you hadn't noticed, there's not a whole lot of altruism in the Jungle.

There is no conflict of interest in doing what you agreed to do for someone *and* getting paid for doing it. In selling real estate, I found that the only conflict is the one created in the seller's mind when it suddenly occurs to him that if he doesn't pay the real estate agent the commission he agreed to, it will mean more chips in *his* pocket. All I did was put a stop to allowing the seller to intimidate me into thinking that my only concern should be *his* welfare, and that being concerned about my own needs was in some way unethical. Such thinking is sheer, intimidating rubbish.

If you're over twenty-one, you are certainly aware that one of the most commonly used intimidation ploys is to make a person feel guilty for concentrating too much on his own well-being. We hear this kind of gibberish from shameless politicians all the time. During election campaigns, they love to rail on endlessly about the disparity between "the rich" and "the poor." Welcome to the world: Of *course* there's a disparity between people at the top of the financial ladder and those at the bottom. There's supposed to be! That's what freedom and free markets are all about. To paraphrase Will Durant, freedom and equality are sworn and everlasting enemies. Nonetheless, political rabble-rousers have been winning the minds of the masses through class-warfare intimidation since the days of the Greek and Roman Empires.

Remember, the Theory of Intimidation states that the results a person achieves are inversely proportionate to the degree to which he is intimidated. By developing techniques to dramatically improve my posture, I positioned myself for accomplishing my ultimate objective—getting paid. In the final analysis, what I really did was separate myself from the rest of the pack by learning how to cope with intimidating people and thereby increasing my chances of actually receiving what I earned.

Specifically, as a closing drew near, I took three important steps to maintain my strong posture:

1. I kept my finger on the pulse of the deal twenty-four hours a day so I could pinpoint the time and place of the closing.

2. I continued to nurture my relationship with the buyer in the hopes that, at a minimum, I would have his moral support.

3. I showed up at the closing with my attorney, and counted on the Universal Attorney-to-Attorney Respect Rule as my insurance policy if all else failed.

If, despite my strong posture and all the precautions I had taken, the seller still tried to cut off my fingers when I reached for my chips, I dispensed with the niceties and drew my mental saber from its sheath. At that point, tactfulness was set aside and it was showdown time. Regardless of whether the seller was trying to steal part or all of my commission, I was militant when it came to protecting my chips.

My attitude was unyielding, solidly backed by the wisdom of the Bluff Theory, which states: *The secret to bluffing is to not bluff.*

In other words, never lay down an ultimatum unless you're prepared to follow through on it. Wealthy people, as you have undoubtedly observed, tend to be excellent bluffers. My Type Number One professor at Screw U. had taught me the importance of financial staying power. He was always prepared to walk away from a deal, because there was no one deal that was life or death to him. If borrowers thought he was bluffing, they did so at their own peril, because he wasn't. When he threatened to walk away from a deal, he meant it. He was always the intimidator, and the prospective borrower either willingly accepted the role of intimidatee or he didn't get the loan. Role assignments were not subject to negotiation with my professor.

If the secret to not bluffing was to have staying power, and if wealth was the backbone of such power, I recognized that I would have to find a substitute for wealth—at least until I reached a point where I possessed significant financial resources. Common sense told me that the only logical substitute for money was determination. The nice thing about determination is that it's just as available to you and me as it is to a billionaire. I simply drew an imaginary line in my gray matter and said to myself, "This is where the intimidation stops. Beyond this line, all bluffs get called."

With determination as my substitute for wealth, if the seller started to reach for my chips, I moved swiftly in an effort to throw a monkey wrench into the closing. It was critical not to get lulled into fiddling while the horse was making a dash for the barn door. If I allowed a closing to occur without getting paid, the problem of securing my chips would become infinitely greater.

If the seller did manage to make it through the closing without paying my commission, and if he continued to refuse to pay me within a short period of time thereafter, I then had no choice but to resort to the one thing I specifically had been trying to avoid from the day I first talked to the seller: legal action. Unfortunately, because of the way the legal system works in the U.S., even the winner of a lawsuit usually ends up losing. Legalman's fee-building techniques virtually guarantee this. But if that was the only course of action left to me, I did not hesitate to take it. I wasn't bluffing.

Thankfully, more often than not things went as planned, and I didn't have to resort to legal action. It was a great feeling to be able to trot into the end zone untouched, and exhilarating to look back over my shoulder and see that no penalty flags had been dropped. Then, and only then, could I delight in watching the points go up on the scoreboard.

At that point—and only at that point—I had completed the final and most important step of selling: *getting paid*. When the game was over, I was not always the most popular guy at the closing, but I had long ago decided that I would rather have the seller taking my name in vain as I walked away with my chips than have him talking about what a nice guy I was as I walked away without my fingers.

In the final chapters of this book, I relate blow-by-blow descriptions of the deals I closed during the first complete year in which I put my reality-based philosophy and techniques into action. These deals resulted in my receiving $849,901 in real estate commissions, yet I was the same tortoise who had barked for a $1,250 bone just a couple of years earlier—with one exception: My shell was now protected by a high-quality intimidation coating.

CHAPTER 15

THE RETURN OF THE TORTOISE

The last time I had ventured into the state of Missouri—almost two years earlier in St. Louis—I returned home demoralized and defeated. I had dared to step out of line and challenge the precedent that it was okay for principals to inflict cruel and unusual punishment on real estate agents. I had scored a touchdown and audaciously suggested that the points be put on the scoreboard. I had been the bad little tortoise who had tried to reach in the cookie jar and ended up getting spanked, the wise-guy real estate agent who had the gall to expect to be paid his full commission just because he had been successful in selling the owner's property at a price that was acceptable to him. It was in St. Louis where I had presumptuously reached for my chips and, as punishment for my crime, had had my entire hand cut off by a white-hatted seller.

It was my devastating experience in St. Louis, more than any other, that had prompted me to vow to find a way to strengthen my posture. I had promised myself that I would leapfrog to a new level and that I would find a way to make certain that in the future I would actually receive what I earned. It was only fitting, then, that less than two years after the low point in my career at Screw U. I should return to the state of Missouri to work on the biggest deal of my life. It was also a nice coincidence that my second Missouri deal happened to approximate the size of my earlier sale in St. Louis.

I first made contact with the three partners (the "Booze Brothers," so called for their unwavering commitment to make hard liquor an integral part of every meeting—morning, noon, and night) who owned the Kansas City properties shortly after making the decision to work full time on large, income-producing real estate. (It is noteworthy to point out that had it not been for the Leapfrog Theory, I never would have pursued the Kansas City deal, because I still would have been focused on second-mortgage loans.) After a couple weeks of analysis and numerous telephone conversations with the Booze Brothers, I decided that the deal looked makeable enough to warrant my investing some serious time and money in it. It goes without saying that I cautioned the Booze Brothers over the phone that I personally would have to inspect the properties before I could "make a commitment."

The best writer in Hollywood could not have put together a more dramatic script. How different it was from my previous experience in Missouri only a short time before. In the St. Louis deal, I had been assured by my Type Number Two professor that his integrity was beyond reproach and that I had no need for a signed commission agreement. His self-righteousness had totally intimidated me. But when I arrived in Kansas City, my posture was very different. I was the expert from afar, and, as such, was pretty much immune to intimidating tactics.

The fact that the eight properties were spread throughout a number of small towns (in both Missouri and Kansas) close to

Kansas City made my inspection task unusually difficult. Luckily, the owners felt there was nothing too good for the expert from afar, so they rented a small, private plane for the inspection tour. That made it possible for me to complete my inspection of all eight apartment developments within twenty-four hours after my arrival. When I finished this meaningless, exhausting tour, there was only one thing I knew for certain: I never again wanted to see another garbage disposal, air-conditioning unit, or cheap wall-to-wall carpeting again.

Then came the big moment—not for me, but the owners. I did some incoherent mumbling, punched a few buttons on my calculator, then played out a dramatic pause that would have made Marlon Brando envious. The owners were in luck. The expert from afar had been satisfied with the inspection, and his calculations had come up positive. While cautioning the Booze Brothers not to become overly optimistic, The Tortoise mercifully let them know that he thought he might be able to "do something" with their properties. There is no greater act of compassion than giving hope to a threesome of alcoholics.

By sheer coincidence, I happened to have eight pre-typed "understandings" with me—one for each property—which I casually pulled from my briefcase at just the right moment. I emphasized that the understandings could, of course, be terminated unilaterally at any time, and that they did not preclude the owners from working with other agents regarding the sale of their properties. Before you could say, "Pardon me, did you say you were a broker?" the understandings were signed and the expert from afar had disappeared across the wheat fields of Missouri. Just who was that scaly green stranger, anyway? Was he for real, or had the owners just been dreaming that an expert from afar had descended upon them? Would he ever return?

Not to worry. The Tortoise's return trips were to be numerous. But first there was an important item that had to be taken care of. While I had obtained one of my three essential legal tools—signed commission agreements for each of the properties—I did not have a real estate license in either Kansas or Missouri. Shortly before I first contacted the Booze Brothers, however, I had inquired about becoming a licensed real estate broker in both states. I had already begun working my way through the massive red tape that had to be dealt with in order to be scheduled to take both real estate brokerage examinations, but at the time I signed the Kansas City agreements I had not yet taken the test in either state.

Once the eight commission agreements were signed, however, it became a top priority to do whatever was necessary to obtain the appropriate licenses. The hard lesson I had previously learned in the Missouri Massacre was still fresh in my mind: A seller is not legally obligated to pay a real estate commission to anyone who is not licensed in the state where the property is located. I had long ago resigned myself to the realities of the government protection racket (i.e., "licensing"), and accepted the fact that the only way to deal with it was to comply.

Accordingly, in the weeks following my initial visit to Kansas City, while working to find prospective buyers for the properties, I also made time to travel to Jefferson City, Missouri and Topeka, Kansas to take the real estate examinations for Missouri and Kansas. Luckily, I passed both tests, and shortly afterward received my real estate brokerage license in both states. I then possessed two of the three legal tools necessary to give real power to my posture, a far cry from the Missouri Massacre in which I had possessed *none* of the necessary legal tools.

The Kansas City deal was a milestone in my career in that it was the first time I had specifically geared all my efforts toward making certain that I got paid if a sale was finalized. Telling friends and acquaintances that I had *closed* another multimillion-dollar deal no longer titillated me. To my chagrin, I found that my grocer and landlord dealt only in cash, not closings. So this time around in Missouri, my main focus was on making certain that I walked away with my chips.

After my first trip to Kansas City, I worked nonstop putting together a detailed, accurate presentation of the Booze Brothers' eight properties, then sent it (by certified mail, of course) to a number of qualified buyers. It was about a month later that I registered (also by certified mail) with the Booze Brothers a real estate investment trust that had showed a great deal of interest in their properties.

After a number of telephone conversations with the president of the real estate investment trust ("Ernest Ego") and the Booze Brothers, Ernest indicated that he was prepared to travel to Kansas City to inspect the properties and meet with the owners. Another inspection—ugh! More garbage disposals, more air-conditioning units, more bricks to stare at. Everyone pretended as though they were intensely interested in every aspect of the tackily constructed apartments, though I had the feeling that the Booze Brothers were just hoping that none of the buildings would collapse during Ernest's obligatory inspection.

Finally, the time came to sit down in the Booze Brothers' office and see if we could structure a deal. The discussions went extraordinarily well, so much so that in a relatively short period of time Ernest was prepared in principle to buy the properties.

When Ernest and I left Kansas City (with my making certain that he boarded his plane before I boarded mine), all *three* entities—i.e., Ernest, the Booze Brothers, *and* The Tortoise—were in agreement on the general terms of the deal. Unlike so many nightmares of the past, it was not just the buyer and seller who had worked out a verbal agreement, while that unnecessary nuisance—the real estate agent—salivated and dutifully waited in the reception room. I had taken charge from the beginning, and every step of the way my focus was on keeping a tight grip on the reigns so I would be in a position to get paid if the sale closed.

It hadn't gone unnoticed by me that, from the outset, Ernest seemed unusually anxious to make the deal. His public company was only a couple years old, but in the past twelve months or so he had made several major acquisitions. In studying his company's annual report, it was clear that if Ernest succeeded in purchasing the eight Kansas City properties, it would elevate his firm from a small, rapidly growing real estate investment trust to a serious force to be reckoned with in the real estate industry. For this reason, it was obvious that he wanted the deal badly.

I therefore sensed that it was the right deal, in the right place, at the right time—and that I was the right tortoise, in the right place, at the right time. For a real estate agent, this is as good as it gets.

First, you have to be prepared; second, you have to find the right opportunity; third, you have to come through at the moment of truth. Most people get plenty of opportunities during their lifetimes, so that's rarely the issue. What counts is how well prepared they are and how good they are at taking advantage of opportunities when they make their appearance. I had been blessed with many excellent opportunities in the past, but had blown them because I wasn't prepared. That, however, was no longer the case. There was no way that I was going to allow myself to be intimidated, because I was now dealing from a posture of strength. My image was strong and, of utmost importance, I had all three legal tools locked safely away in my files.

In addition, I had done an outstanding job of securing all the information Ernest had requested in the performance of his due diligence, and I was now following through on every detail. Was it possible, I wondered to myself, that it was meant for me to return to Missouri—the state where the St. Louis debacle had occurred—to prove that I finally understood how to handle the master intimidators of the Business World Jungle? Could there actually be justice for reptiles in a world infested by white-hatted humanoids?

After a couple more weeks of hammering out the details via telephone, we all (again, me included) decided that it was time to meet in Kansas City and try to finalize the terms of a sale. This time, however, there were three additional parties involved in the transaction: the Booze Brothers' attorney, Ernest Ego's attorney, and—you guessed it—The Tortoise's attorney!

By now, nothing that the expert from afar did could surprise either Ernest or the Booze Brothers, but it was difficult for their attorneys to fathom the idea of a real estate agent being represented by an attorney at a closing. Truly, these were uncharted waters for Legalman.

I, of course, went through the formality of properly acknowledging all of Legalman's normal deal-killing goodies as "points" that would have to be "handled" so we could get on with the closing. When appropriate, I stated (*not* asked) as many ways as possible that we (*not* just Legalman) would (*not* could) handle (*not* solve) the particular points (*not* problems) in question.

I should also point out that I had some help in finessing my way around Legalman. As previously stated, I had determined from the outset that Ernest was anxious to make a deal in order to speed up the elevation of his company to a more exalted status. The price he indicated he was willing to pay was, in my opinion, considerably in excess of the true market value of the properties. Interestingly, though, the price we had been discussing was still considerably less than the original asking price of the principals, which again emphasized the reality that a seller never gives his true price at the outset.

Though they came across as "Aw, shucks" cowboys, the fact is that the Booze Brothers were no dummies. Above all, they were excellent actors, and they knew full well that the price we were talking about—approximately $2.7 million over and above the combined mortgages—was a golden opportunity to unload their cardboard-and-scotch-tape apartment complexes at a huge profit.

Being superb salesmen themselves, the Booze Brothers, for effect, continued to cry the blues and complain about the price all through the negotiations. However, while putting on an admittedly convincing show, their desire to close the deal could be seen in their actions, and that desire was critical to my being able to offset the Attorney Goal Line Defense. I felt pretty certain that behind closed doors they were tossing Legalman biscuits and trying to keep him in his cage. Oscar-winning performances of dissatisfaction notwithstanding, it was obvious they were anxious to finalize the sale.

I can't tell you how much I enjoyed witnessing the Booze Brothers performances. I'd rather watch an experienced real estate developer hype, con, and lie his way through a deal than sit on the fifty yard line at a Super Bowl game. And when you're lucky enough to get three of them together in one deal, they feed on each other's performances much like great Broadway stars. To this day, I still admire their professionalism (as actors, not real estate developers).

Nonetheless, I felt secure with the Booze Brothers, because I recognized them as Type Number Ones. From the outset, they had made it clear that the name of the game was to get the best possible deal for themselves, and I appreciated their candor. As I explained earlier, if you're prepared when you deal with a Type Number One, he's the least dangerous of all Jungle creatures. You always know exactly where you stand with him, which gives you the opportunity to implement whatever precautionary measures you deem necessary.

The negotiations and legal documentation went on for three days, night and day, and had everyone walking around in a stupor from mental and physical exhaustion. On the second day, notwithstanding my strong posture, the Booze Brothers began to hint that there might be a need to perform the usual commissiondectomy. (Those readers who sell real estate for a living are no doubt familiar with the term *commissiondectomy*. It is a delicate surgical procedure aimed at removing all or part of a real estate agent's commission from his grasp. Sadly, most real estate agents practically volunteer for this painful operation by leaving their commissions unprotected and exposed to the avaricious appetites of Jungle predators.)

The Booze Brothers pointed out that Ernest and they were still several hundred thousand dollars apart, with no apparent way of closing the gap. It seemed to them that the only way the deal could be put together was for The Tortoise to be more

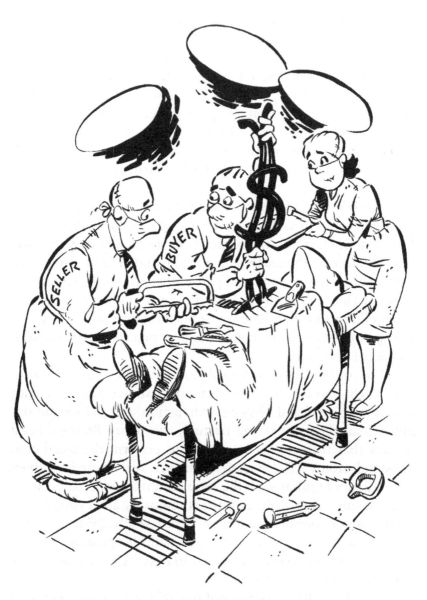

*"It's getting harder and harder to remove
these things from reptiles."*

"reasonable" with regard to his commission, but I quickly assured all parties that I had no interest in submitting to a commission-dectomy procedure.

To my dismay, however, my tough stance did not seem to ruffle anyone, and I was pretty certain that I knew the reason for their confidence. All the parties were fully aware of two of the legal tools I had in my bag—signed commission agreements for the eight properties and certified mail registering Ernest's company as the buyer—but they undoubtedly assumed that The Tortoise was not licensed to sell real estate in either Kansas or Missouri. After all, it would have been unheard of for anyone to have the foresight—let alone the willingness to spend the time and money—to make his way through all the red tape, apply for real estate brokerage licenses in two faroff states, study the real estate licensing laws of those states, then travel thousands of miles to take the required examinations and become ordained by their state governments.

No question about it, their assumption was reasonable. It definitely was unheard of for someone to go to such extremes—unless, of course, that someone was a relentless tortoise who had undergone a major commissiondectomy in the very same state less than two years earlier.

Though I can never prove it, I have always believed that between the second and third days of our closing meetings in Kansas City, the Booze Brothers' attorney, as a formality, checked with the Kansas and Missouri Real Estate Commissions to confirm that I was not a licensed broker in either state. The reason for my belief is that the atmosphere changed dramatically when we met on the third day. Here they were—Ernest, the Booze Brothers, and their respective attorneys—in the midst of what appeared to be a routine commissiondectomy, when, on the third day, everyone suddenly seemed to be very concerned about my unwillingness to submit to the operation.

As the hours passed, increasing time and attention were devoted to the commission "problem," with more and more of the conversation being directed at my attorney and me. To their dismay, however, we didn't budge an inch. I was fascinated by how an agreed-upon-in-advance payment for a job well done could be verbally transformed into a "problem." I kept wondering what word they would have used to describe the situation had I *not* produced a buyer for their ticky-tacky properties.

The attorneys worked into the early hours of the morning to get the documentation in order and sort out all the legal details related to the sale of the eight major properties. Secretaries typed away frantically, copying machines ran continuously, and a variety of strange people dashed in and out of the Booze Brothers' attorney's offices to sign mysterious documents.

When we finally stopped working at the end of the third day, it was two o'clock in the morning and everyone was thoroughly exhausted. Ernest, the Booze Brothers, my attorney, and I went back to the motel where we were all staying. (The Booze Brothers lived in Lawrence, Kansas, but the closing was scheduled to take place in Kansas City, Missouri, so they, too, were staying overnight.) As we climbed the stairs on the way to our second-floor rooms, Ernest suggested that we all come to his room "to relax and kick around a few points."

Now, I might be a tortoise, but I'm not so slow that it wasn't obvious to me that Ernest, following another grueling, sixteen-hour workday, had better things to do at two o'clock in the morning than just "relax and kick around a few points" with a trio of drunks and a guy walking around with a shell on this back.

As we climbed the stairs, I thought to myself, "This is it. You've waited almost two years for this moment. You've endured endless frustration and humiliation, but, in typical tortoise fashion, you kept trudging ahead. You studied, you analyzed, you planned, you followed through. And this time you're prepared. It's clear that the ball is going to go over the goal line; the only question is whether or not you're going to get credit for the score. And that's going to be determined by whether or not you allow yourself to be intimidated, make a last-minute mistake, and have the touchdown called back. You have to play it cool, remember that the only way to bluff is to not bluff, and have the self-discipline and determination to do the right thing rather than yield to the temptation to act on emotion."

As I entered Ernest's room, I reminded myself that nothing about this deal had happened by accident, and I mentally vowed that I would maintain control of the situation to assure that no last-minute penalties occurred. Before describing what took place in Ernest's room, however, I should point out that there was another significant factor in this deal. In addition to the approximately 1,250 apartment units that made up the eight properties, Ernest and the Booze Brothers planned to enter into a contingent agreement for Ernest's company to purchase nearly 1,000 additional units that were to be built in the near future.

It was unclear as to whether I, as the licensed real estate broker who had initially brought Ernest and the Booze Brothers together, would be entitled to a commission on these additional properties if and when a deal was consummated. When I had originally discussed the eight properties with Ernest, I also pointed out to him the possibility of purchasing additional units to be built in the future, so I certainly had a reasonable claim to a commission on these properties. However, up until the meeting in his motel room, everyone involved, including myself, had conspicuously avoided talking about where The Tortoise stood with regard to the to-be-built units.

After we assembled in Ernest's room, the Booze Brothers went through a continuation of their Oscar-worthy performances about how much of their own cash they had put into the building of their apartment developments (even though later, many months after the closing, they laughingly told me how they had, in fact, *overfinanced* the projects—meaning they had actually put money into their pockets from the financing they had obtained for construction) and how they would barely realize a profit from the sale as it was now structured.

Ernest made it clear that he had already agreed to a higher price than he should have (and he was absolutely right), and appealed to my rationality. There was no way that the deal could stand a $375,000 commission (3 percent of approximately $12.5 million). Surely, The Tortoise would not blow up a sale of this magnitude by refusing to accept a commission in the range of $150,000 to $200,000. Real estate agents just weren't supposed to make $375,000 on one deal. My impertinence was galling. Worse, I couldn't even seem to conjure up the decency to feel guilty.

It was, in fact, the defining moment that sooner or later arrives in every contest in life, whether business or personal: To be or not to be intimidated?

Even though I still had a strong posture, in no small way aided by my having the right legal tools on my side, Ernest and the Booze Brothers were counting on my sanity and logic. Surely I would not be crazy enough to throw away the opportunity to earn a handsome, six-figure commission; surely I would see the logic in taking a $150,000 commission rather than no commission at all.

But Ernest and the Booze Brothers knew nothing about my undergraduate days at Screw U. Or about my previous crucifixion in the Missouri Massacre. Or about my agonizing wait of almost two years for this very moment to occur. Or about the fact that nothing in this deal had happened by accident. Or about my being well aware that this was the *right* seller and the *right* buyer in the *right* place at the *right* time.

It was the perfect situation, one I had long dreamed about. It was time to put it all on the line. It was time to bluff by not bluffing. It was time to go for the touchdown and not be intimidated into settling for a cowardly field goal. It was time to suck it in and hang tough. My determination was unwavering. I had taken my stand, and there would be no backing down. I could almost hear the crowds chanting, "Green Power! Green Power!"

After repeated, vain attempts to try to get me to come to my senses, Ernest and the Booze Brothers began to get testy. Timing is a critical factor in every deal, and I knew that the time was right for my now historic speech: *The Tortoise Briefcase Address*. In a deadpan, matter-of-fact manner, I said, "Boys, there's no sense going around in circles all night. It looks like we aren't going to be able work this deal out, so let's just write if off to experience. Hey, it's not the last deal in the world."

I then looked at Ernest and said, "Don't worry, I'm working on a lot of other properties. Sooner or later, I'll come across a deal for you where the mathematics make sense." I then turned to the Booze Brothers and said, "As to your properties, I've been talking to several other prospective buyers, and I think I can crank up some serious interest in the next couple of weeks." (You can just imagine how happy Ernest was to hear *that*.)

I then put my papers back in my briefcase, closed it, and snapped the latches shut—*very* slowly—one latch at a time. Then I rose, smiled pleasantly, started toward the door, paused, glanced back over my shoulder, and, in the most cavalier manner, said, "Why don't you guys get some sleep. I'll be in touch with you in the next couple of weeks."

I was conscious of my every move and every word as I completed The Tortoise Briefcase Address in a style that rivaled some of the Booze Brothers' greatest performances. I will always remember the distance—I was approximately three feet from the door—when Ernest and the Booze Brothers yelled out, in unison, "Wait!" That was the most telltale word anyone had ever spoken to me. That one word confirmed that I had been right all along—that this was the right buyer and the right seller in the right place at the right time.

What Ernest had meant by that one word was that there was no way, after all the effort he had put into this deal, that he was going to miss the opportunity to propel his company into a significant real estate investment trust just because some real estate broker happened to be crazy.

As for the Booze Brothers, the word *wait* was their way of saying that there was no way, after all the work they had done, that they were going to miss the opportunity to pocket more than $2 million profit just because some real estate broker was too stupid to understand the consequences of his actions.

Unbeknownst to either Ernest or the Booze Brothers, from the outset of this deal I had operated under the assumption that I would never receive a dime for the sale of the to-be-built units. First, I realized that there was at least a reasonable argument that I was not legally entitled to a commission on those units. Second, I've never had any faith in contingent closings. How was I to know if the apartments would ever be built, and, even if they were, how could I be sure that Ernest would ever complete the purchase? And the way the Brothers Booze drank, how could I be certain they would even live that long? (Sadly, one of them did pass away not too many years after the closing.)

I again made it clear that there was absolutely no negotiation regarding my 3 percent commission for the sale of the eight properties. However, "in a show of good faith to try to help pull this deal together," I said that I would consider taking an *additional* $50,000 cash right now in lieu of any future commission on the units to be completed and purchased at a later date. In other words, I was going to give the Booze Brothers (and, theoretically, Ernest) the opportunity to save several hundred thousand dollars (my potential commission) down the road by coming up with an additional $50,000 right now.

When Ernest and the Booze Brothers came out of the ether, the commission we finally agreed upon as a *compromise* was $426,901.39—about $50,000 *more* than the approximately $375,000 commission I had been shooting for. Let me tell you, that kind of compromise made up for a lot of past commissiondectomies.

In the end, Ernest Ego and the Booze Brothers structured the Kansas City deal so there would be two closings, aside and apart from the contingent purchase of the to-be-built apartments for which I had agreed to forfeit any claims to a commission. Four of the properties were closed immediately, for which I received a commission of $221,446.50. The second closing, for the remaining four apartment developments, was set for two months hence, and would result in my receiving an additional commission of $205,454.89.

When I had vowed to leapfrog to a new level and find a way to actually pocket what I earned, I had no idea that I would return to Missouri soil to make good on my vows. It was a great ending for what easily could have been a movie script. Happily, though, it wasn't a script; it was real life. For the first time, I had experienced the thrill of a major victory over big-league intimidators.

Driving over the bridge separating downtown Kansas City from the old airport, my commission check safely locked away in my briefcase, my attorney looked over at me and asked, "Well, how do you feel?"

Without hesitating, I looked at him and replied, "Deserving."

CHAPTER 16

THE RETURN OF THE TORTOISE, PART II

The second Kansas City closing, like all closings, had more than its share of problems. For starters, much of the dirty laundry that normally comes to the surface just prior to a closing predictably did not show up until after the first Kansas City sale was consummated. With each new surprise, Ernest Ego became increasingly upset with the Booze Brothers and more hesitant about closing on the second group of apartments.

About two weeks before the scheduled second closing, Ernest's attorney sent a letter to the Booze Brothers' attorney in which he stated that before the second closing could take place, the dirty laundry discovered since the first closing would have to be cleaned up. He enclosed a copy of a letter from Ernest that listed no less than twenty-nine unpleasant surprises he had been confronted with since taking over the first four properties. I suddenly had visions of my additional $205,000+ commission going down the drain along with the Booze Brothers' dirty laundry.

The next day, Ernest's attorney sent another letter to the Booze Brothers' attorney, this one listing a number of legal and tax problems he had discovered since the first closing. I had a feeling that Ernest's attorney, at his direction, was reaching into his bag of deal-killing goodies to gum up the works, because Ernest was probably looking for a way to back out of the second closing.

From my standpoint, there was too much at stake to allow Legalman to destroy the second closing, so I rolled up my sleeves and worked around the clock to try to resolve the problems and pull the deal back together. I employed every psychological tool at my disposal to try to keep peace between Ernest and the Booze Brothers. Things were becoming very heated between them, and the Booze Brothers made it clear to me that they felt they had a valid purchase agreement with Ernest for the second group of properties. They also made it clear that they were going to institute a massive lawsuit against Ernest's company if he did not go through with the second closing.

I was experienced enough by this time to know that the worst possible way to try to get the other side to accede to your wishes is to make hostile threats, so I urged the Booze Brothers not to threaten Ernest with a lawsuit. I reminded them that there was big money involved, and that threats would only succeed in provoking Ernest into taking a tougher stand. If you push a person to the point where he feels that he has to stand his ground in order to save face—sort of a knee-jerk, macho response—emotion tends to overrule logic.

I told the Booze Brothers that I would set up a conference call with Ernest, and that if we all kept calm and worked together, the "points" (that old standby word for "problems") in question could be "handled." I then made a separate call to Ernest and assured him that the Booze Brothers were honorable people and had only the best of intentions. I said that even though the Booze

Brothers had not mentioned the possibility of a lawsuit to me (which, of course, they had), I suspected that it was only a matter of time until Legalman would suggest that they institute legal proceedings if the second closing did not take place on schedule. I painted a gruesome picture of a New Yorker coming to Missouri or Kansas, or both—Booze Brothers' turf—and trying to win a lawsuit against a bunch of wholesome (to the extent hard liquor can be considered to be wholesome) country boys.

I further reminded him what a great public relations roll his company was on, and that he should consider what a lawsuit might do to his company's image. The first Kansas City purchase had given him a lot of favorable publicity, and the public was taking note of the fact that his company was growing rapidly. I opined that with the company's stock climbing as it had been, the possibility of a major lawsuit and the attendant bad publicity could knock the props out from under its market value. In addition, I pointed out that negative publicity could be a hindrance to his acquiring other properties in the future.

Finally, I told Ernest that because the Booze Brothers were reasonable people, there was no question in my mind that the "points" he had discovered since the first closing could be easily "handled" if we worked together in a spirit of cooperation. I then let him know that I was going to set up a conference call with the Booze Brothers so we could proceed with "ironing out the details."

By giving the same pacification speech to both sides, I managed to diffuse a potentially explosive situation. I made each party believe that the mind-set of the other party was cooperative and reasonable, a mind-set they had not been willing to display when talking directly to each other. Now that I had changed their perceptions of each other's attitude, I felt it was safe to move forward with a conference call.

The call worked like a charm. During the discussion, both Ernest and the Booze Brothers talked in a cooperative spirit, with no sign whatsoever of hostilities. We calmly reviewed the twenty-nine points on Ernest's list and discussed the best way to resolve each one of them. Compromise proved to be the order of the day. It was agreed that as soon as the Booze Brothers had taken care of the items they promised to correct, the second closing would commence. Sure enough, within a week, both sides were satisfied and prepared to close the second group of apartments.

I should add that there was another fairly significant change that took place between the first and second Kansas City closings. The Leapfrog Theory had worked spectacularly well for me, and I was determined to move onward and upward. Now that I had succeeded in leapfrogging over the rest of the pack, I wanted to go even higher, so high that future closings would be even smoother than my first Kansas City closing had been with regard to receiving my commission.

And higher I went—about 41,000 feet higher. In a fit of youthful impulsiveness, I purchased a Learjet (on credit, of course)—long before Gulfstreams had become commonplace toys for every corporate executive worth his salt. My rationale for making such an elephantine purchase was two-pronged: (1) It would be an efficient tool that would allow me to be personally involved in many more deals simultaneously, and (2) it would add considerably to my posture and make it even more difficult for buyers and sellers to intimidate me.

In retrospect, the former was a more defensible rationale than the latter, because there's no question that a private plane is a remarkable efficiency tool. As to my strong-posture rationale, however, while my Learjet was an effective prop in this regard, from a cash-flow standpoint a private jet is a bit more suited to a Fortune 500 board chairman than a real estate broker. Nevertheless, being the young, impetuous tortoise I was, I financially obligated myself to the ultimate overhead hog.

My arrival for the second Kansas City closing was a real-life enactment of every real estate agent's wildest fantasy. This was one time that I did not fly with the buyer to the seller's city, nor did I even concern myself with arriving in Kansas City ahead of the buyer. By the day of the closing, both Ernest and the Booze Brothers had been made aware of the fact that the expert from afar had purchased a private jet, and I had made arrangements ahead of time to have them meet me at the Kansas City airport. (Try to get a buyer and seller to do *that* if you're a real estate agent flying commercially!)

The setting was like something out of a Woody Allen movie. Ernest and one of the Booze Brothers were sitting in the coffee shop of the main terminal at a table next to the window. Nicely, this gave them a perfect view of the airport's main runway. There they were, drinking coffee and waiting for—of all people—the *broker* to arrive! A new precedent had been set for the relationship between buyer, seller, and broker.

Suddenly, from out of the clouds streaked a shiny, blue-and-white Learjet, its jet engines screaming through the skies as it descended toward the runway. Ernest Ego and the Booze Brother watched as my Learjet touched down, then taxied to a private aviation hangar. The expert from afar, who was really nothing more than a good real estate broker who had learned the art of handling intimidators, had arrived. The closing could now proceed.

Need I say that there were no late-night motel-room discussions this time around? The closing went smoothly, and I walked away with another $205,454.89 as my commission for the second phase of the Kansas City sale.

This time, as we went over the bridge on the way to the airport, my attorney asked me, "Well, how do you feel *now?*"

I thought about it for a moment, then looked at him and answered, "Intimidating."

P.S. Not only did Ernest Ego never buy the second phase (i.e., the to-be-built apartments), but the Booze Brothers, who, notwithstanding their windfall profits, got into serious financial trouble shortly after the second closing, never succeeded in building the additional units. Last I heard they were seen standing on a street corner and carrying signs that read: Will Develop Real Estate for Food.

And Ernest Ego? Like so many real estate investment trusts of those early years, his company ultimately ended up in bankruptcy. It all served as a grim reminder to me that the all-show-and-no-dough game is never-ending.

"Hey, guys, why not toss in the towel and give Hollywood a try instead?"

CHAPTER 17

THE TORTOISE
DONS HIS HARE COSTUME

After the Kansas City textbook illustration of how to apply my reality-based philosophy to big-money deals, I inexcusably deviated from my own rules and managed to find a way to get burned again. The setting for this sad Tortoise tale was Dayton, Ohio. It was obvious from the beginning that the main principal in the Dayton deal ("Mr. Biggshotte") was a classic Type Number One, so there was no excuse for letting my guard down.

It was a difficult deal, because I had to invest an inordinate amount of effort into getting my commission agreement signed, which should have alerted me to trouble on the horizon. After several discussions with Mr. Biggshotte, he informed me that his property was actually owned by a limited partnership and that he was one of the three general partners. He assured me, however, that he "controlled the deal" and that there would be no problem.

When Mr. Biggshotte finally signed my commission agreement, he inserted a handwritten clause at the bottom of the last page that stated that the agreement was not valid unless executed by his two partners. He assured me that this was merely a "gesture of respect" so as not to offend his Washington, D.C., partner ("Sam Sewage") by making it look as though he had entered into a deal without his knowledge. Mr. Biggshotte also assured me that Sam Sewage would do whatever he asked him to do. Further, he told me that even if his partner refused to sign the agreement, he still possessed the legal authority to bind the partnership. The bottom line was that Mr. Biggshotte verbally guaranteed me that he would make the commission agreement valid with or without Sam Sewage's signature.

Mr. Biggshotte then called Sam Sewage and set up an appointment for me to come to Washington to talk to him in person. The next day, I flew to D.C. and, shades of my early days at Screw U., spent a couple of hours sitting in Sam's reception room, waiting for him to see me. Finally, my self-respect came to my rescue. I asked myself how in the world I had gotten into a situation where I was again sitting dutifully in some rude monger's reception room, waiting for him to bless me with a few minutes of his valuable time.

Having come to my senses, I got up, walked over to the receptionist's desk, and asked her if I could use the telephone. I then called Mr. Biggshotte and told him that I was going to leave unless Sam Sewage met with me immediately. Mr. Biggshotte tried to calm me down, and assured me that he would call Sam as soon as I got off the line.

Sure enough, within a few minutes Sam Sewage granted me an audience. I restrained my urge to spill a bottle of Liquid Paper on his powder-blue polyester suit, and instead suggested that we go over the details of the deal. After a few minutes of prefacing remarks, I explained the commission agreement to him, but, to my dismay, Sam said that he would need a day or two to study the agreement before signing. Though he emphasized that he didn't see anything wrong with the agreement, he said that, as a matter of principle, he didn't like to "rush into things."

I was pretty fed up after having to sit in Sam's waiting room so long, particularly after traveling all the way to Washington, so I was not about to lower myself and try to pressure him into signing against his will. Instead, I acted casual and told him to look over the agreement and get back to Mr. Biggshotte when he was ready to sign.

On the way home, one of those fateful coincidences of life occurred. During an hour's layover at the Pittsburgh airport (my Learjet was down for repairs), I bumped into none other than the third partner in the deal ("Eddie Enigma"). I was never quite certain exactly what Eddie contributed to the partnership. He had no real estate expertise, had apparently done none of the work with regard to the financing or building of the project, and, I was told, had liquid assets that would make dinner at Taco Bell a challenge for him. Mr. Biggshotte had simply told me that Eddie was not a factor in the deal and that I should just ignore him.

On the flight home, I told Eddie that I had just come from Washington and that, although Sam Sewage had not yet signed the agreement, he had assured me that he would do so shortly. I then showed him several copies of the agreement, which contained Mr. Biggshotte's signature, and suggested that he also may as well sign it since it was not valid anyway until Sam Sewage signed.

Surprisingly, Eddie Enigma actually signed the document as per my request, so I was now missing only Sam Sewage's signature. At this point, I was pretty confident, because all the evidence indicated that Mr. Biggshotte really was the one who was in control of the deal. Regardless, he had already promised me that he would honor my commission agreement even if Sam Sewage refused to sign it.

As you might have guessed, after reviewing the agreement for a few days, Sam Sewage did, in fact, refuse to sign it. Notwithstanding, Mr. Biggshotte urged me to proceed with working on a sale of the Dayton property. He deleted the clause he had added at the bottom of the agreement regarding the other partners' signatures, then initialed the deletion. (At a later date, I also got Eddie Enigma to initial the deletion.) Mr. Biggshotte explained that he and Eddie controlled more than two-thirds of the partnership, and, as a result, they had the legal power to bind it and enter into an agreement with me.

Even though the agreement was not as ironclad as I would have liked, I decided to move forward with working on a sale of the Dayton apartment development anyway. There were three reasons for my decision.

First, as I pointed out, from all indications it appeared that Mr. Biggshotte really was in control of the deal, which even Eddie Enigma had confirmed, and it was Mr. Biggshotte with whom I was dealing.

Second, in order for a sale to be consummated, Sam Sewage would have to sign the closing documents, and his signing would be de-facto proof that he did, in fact, approve of the terms of the sale.

Third, I was on strong legal ground, because I was licensed to sell real estate in Ohio, and, in addition, I planned to make certain that there would be plenty of certified mail in my files as evidence of my involvement. In fact, the real estate laws in Ohio, like most states, protected the "procuring broker" even if he only had a verbal agreement.

As always, I gathered extensive data on the property and put together an impressive package. This soon led to a serious interest on the part of the same company that had purchased the St. Louis apartment development where I had undergone my most painful commissiondectomy. My contact at that company ("Arnold Apathy") was also the same person with whom I had negotiated the St. Louis deal, which should have been another red flag for me had I not been sleepwalking. After all, Arnold had spoken nary a word on my behalf when my Type Number Two professor severed my fingers in the Missouri Massacre. Looking back on it now, it's hard for me to believe that I moved forward with working on this deal with the knowledge that there were potential problems with both the buyer *and* seller. My only excuse is that this deal took place many years before I had undergone my first brain-transplant surgery.

It goes without saying that I sent the deal to Arnold Apathy by certified mail, and that I also registered his company by certified mail with Mr. Biggshotte. Before inspecting the property, however, Arnold sent an outline of an offer to me, and asked that I have the seller sign it if it was acceptable. It was a reasonable offer—$800,000 over the mortgage, subject only to Arnold's inspection of the property—and I was successful in getting Mr. Biggshotte to sign it.

About a week later, Arnold Apathy came to Dayton to inspect the property. It was the usual, meaningless staring at bricks, touring of bathrooms and laundry rooms, looking down garbage disposals, and opening closet doors. Arnold let it be known that he was satisfied with what he had seen, and at that point I thought we were headed for a quick closing.

Mr. Biggshotte, who had let me know from the outset that he was in desperate financial straits, said that the only way he was interested in going through with the deal was if the buyer could close it right away. So, to expedite the handling of the myriad details that would have to be taken care of before a closing could occur, Mr. Biggshotte and I flew to New York a couple weeks later to meet personally with Arnold Apathy.

It was during that New York trip that I began to get lulled into a false sense of security. Even before we went to New York, Mr. Biggshotte and I had become pretty chummy, and he continually praised me for the great job I was doing in handling all aspects of the deal. He told me point blank that he had never seen a real estate broker do such a thorough, efficient job and be

"Gosh—real, live bricks. I'm overwhelmed."

so aggressive in moving a deal forward. In fact, he lavished so much praise on me that, much like my eternal nemesis, the hare, I began to relax and think to myself, "How sweet it is." I hadn't experienced this kind of infatuation since my White-Hatted professor at Screw U. flunked me in Holier-Than-Thou 101.

Another reason for our buddy-buddy relationship was that I liked Mr. Biggshotte's candor. He didn't exactly have a sterling reputation, which was understandable given that he was an extreme Type Number One who had no qualms about trying to grab both his *and* everyone else's chips. During one of our conversations, when he and I were chatting about business philosophy, he said to me, "Let's face it, in business every guy grabs his best hold and goes for all he can get, any way he can get it. Everything else is B.S." This hardly shocked me, considering what I had been through both during and after my days at Screw U. How could I deny that there was a certain amount of truth to what he was saying, considering my firsthand experience with disorganized crime in the Jungle. It wasn't the way I wished things would be, but the way I had to admit they really were.

During our New York trip, Mr. Biggshotte and I tied the bow around our romance. He continued to praise me, and I continued to lap up every word. Ignoring reality and displaying a shocking ability to rationalize away the facts, I figured I had nothing to fear, because I not only possessed an Ohio real estate license, a signed commission agreement with Mr. Biggshotte and Eddie Enigma, and plenty of certified-mail slips as proof of my involvement, I also had the advantage of knowing Mr. Biggshotte's business philosophy. My impeccable lack of logic was analogous to a person deciding that even though he had advance word that armed bandits were going to rob a bank within the next five minutes, it was safe for him to go inside because he was wearing a bullet-proof vest.

About two weeks after our New York trip, Arnold Apathy sent me a purchase agreement for the Dayton property. To be sure, the fact that all mail and communications were being channeled through me gave me a great sense of security. Mr. Biggshotte continued to praise me for the outstanding job I was doing, and Arnold Apathy displayed considerably more respect for my position in this deal than he had in the Missouri Massacre. It looked like a slam-dunk.

As we got nearer to a closing, however, Arnold Apathy demanded that Mr. Biggshotte supply a considerable amount of additional information. As usual, I took matters into my own hands and did most of the work. In fact, in this particular deal my staff and I took care of things that normally could be handled only by a seller's own personnel. With his blessing, my staff virtually took over Mr. Biggshotte's office and provided such information as rent rolls, tax bills, and a long list of other items that required exhausting hours and numerous trips to Dayton.

Finally, the day arrived when Arnold Apathy was satisfied and ready for a closing. Because of Mr. Biggshotte's desperation, the Attorney Goal Line Defense was almost nonexistent in this deal. Legalman probably figured that the only way he would ever get his bill paid by Mr. Biggshotte was to actually help (blasphemy!) get the deal closed. Witnessing Legalman wave aside problems is about as common as viewing Halley's Comet.

On the day of the scheduled closing, one of the more common dirty-laundry problems surfaced. The insurance company that held the mortgage on the property refused to allow a transfer of the apartment development to the buyer. The insurance company was unhappy with Mr. Biggshotte because of his delinquent mortgage payments, rent rolls they had found to be less than accurate, and a number of other questionable items. Here I was on the one yard line, a commission of approximately $97,000 within my grasp, and from out of nowhere the insurance company was threatening to gum up the works by refusing to allow the sale to go through.

What to do? My old standby, of course: Take matters into my own hands. I flew to Cincinnati (where the insurance company was located) with *my* attorney and Mr. Biggshotte. What transpired at the insurance company's office that day was like something out of a soap opera. Mr. Biggshotte begged almost to the point of tears, but the insurance company's executive henchmen stood firm. My attorney tried a tactful approach, but to no avail. I appealed to their powers of reason. Forget it. It was obvious that the boys in the pinstripe suits didn't have a great deal of sympathy for sociopathic real estate developers.

It didn't make any sense to me. Here was an opportunity for them to get rid of Mr. Biggshotte, Sam Sewage, and Eddie Enigma, all of whom they obviously disdained, and secure a substantial real estate company in their place. So where was their logic? Foolish tortoise that I was, it didn't occur to me that what the insurance company was angling for was quite simple: Blood!

The next time you walk by one of those beautiful insurance company skyscrapers, remember that all that glass and steel you see is held together by dried, human blood. These are the same insurance companies who run those upbeat ads on television, the ones where their friendly agents are always helping out some traumatized neighborhood family. Insurance companies may seem stuffy to most of us, but they know all the angles. They've been around since the Stone Age, and have seen (and tried) every trick. Insurance company executives know all about Mr. Biggshotte's Jungle philosophy of grabbing your best hold and going for everything you can get. They also routinely crush hotshot real estate developers like Mr. Biggshotte without giving it a second thought.

Finally, out of the goodness of their hearts, the insurance company's foot soldiers decided that they were going to allow Mr. Biggshotte to donate a couple pints of blood in exchange for approving the transfer of his property. After more begging, tears, and hard-luck stories, Mr. Biggshotte begrudgingly agreed to allow the insurance company to stick the needle in his arm and draw the required amount of blood under the euphemism of "mortgage transfer fee."

After we left the insurance company's offices, Mr. Biggshotte, though bitter about being forced to make a donation to the insurance company's blood bank, was also elated that the sale could now be closed. He had been on the verge of losing the deal, but it now looked like it was going to be finalized. Mr. Biggshotte gushed all over me and my attorney, telling us how grateful he was for what we had done for him and that he would never forget it. To his credit, he admitted that without us he didn't believe that he would have been able to get the insurance company to agree to the transfer. Bottom line: Without me, he would have had no deal and the project would have ended up in Busted Projects Heaven.

Such gratefulness was pure ecstasy for me, so much so that I quickly stepped inside a phone booth and changed into my tattered hare costume, which I hadn't used in years. It was like turning against my own people ... er, reptiles. There was no more need to be on guard, thought I, because any fool could see that the deal was in the bag. Rather than being focused on my commission, one would have thought that my main concern was in seeing to it that nothing got in the way of my flaming romance with Mr. Biggshotte. The gushing, the praise, and the back-slapping was so intense that it bordered on amorous. So much so that I told my attorney that he need not accompany us to the closing. I had, in fact, totally lost my mind!

So off to Dayton I went with my new best friend, Mr. Biggshotte, who continued to talk as though he owed his very life to me. But, alas, this time it was I who went under the ether. Shades of my performance in Victor Vermin's reception room in Cincinnati years earlier: The last thing I remembered was waiting around in an attorney's reception room, sucking my thumb and playing with my yo-yo while the closing was taking place in another room. Finally, Mr. Biggshotte came bustling out of the closing room and announced that everything was "done" and that "we're all going out to dinner to celebrate."

Swift-witted soul that I was, I timidly asked Mr. Biggshotte, "Uh, what about my commission?" "Don't worry about it," my newfound best friend retorted, "I'm taking care of everything." "Gosh," I thought to myself, "and for a moment there I thought I might have a problem." Mr. Biggshotte seemed so jubilant that I hated to do anything to dampen his spirits, so I decided not to press him. Mother Teresa would have been proud of my compassionate mind-set.

All parties to the closing were at the victory celebration dinner—Mr. Biggshotte, Sam Sewage, Arnold Apathy, their attorneys, and, yes, even Eddie Enigma. From my standpoint, Sam Sewage was the key to the deal, because by signing the closing documents, he, in effect, had made a legal representation that he approved of the sale.

Even at the celebration dinner, Mr. Biggshotte continued to heap praise on me in front of everyone. I was so flattered that I was tempted to pull out my yo-yo and perform a couple new tricks I had learned in the reception room while everyone else had been busy with more mundane matters—like closing the sale. Everything was quite lovely until I happened to notice that the first course being served was turtle soup, which finally jolted me out of my sedation. It's wonderful being invited to dinner, but not when you're on the menu!

Finally, it all started coming back to me—my years at Screw U., my past experiences in the Jungle, the defensive techniques I had developed. I reminded myself that I had been dealing with an archetypal Type Number One, a nasty Jungle predator who had made it clear to me from the outset that the name of the game was to get as many chips as possible by whatever means necessary. "Mustn't panic," I thought to myself. I had to find a way to talk to Mr. Biggshotte in private as quickly as possible.

After about an hour, Mr. Biggshotte excused himself to go to the men's room. This was my big chance. I, too, excused myself, but no one bothered to even acknowledge me. It was as though I were invisible. My separation from the closing had been carried

*"Hold up on the praise, sweetheart, while I slip
into something more suitable for the occasion."*

out with such grace and finesse that most of the celebrants probably wondered what I was doing at the dinner. For them, it was a celebration; for me, it was the last supper.

The men's room wasn't my idea of an ideal place to conduct business, but I had no choice. By this time, I had shed my hare costume and, as a true tortoise again, was determined to get to the crux of the issue right then and there. It's not easy to act casual when you're standing next to a urinal and watching someone relieve himself, but I tried my best. I told Mr. Biggshotte that I didn't want to ruin his celebration, but that I had not yet received my commission.

Then came the now-famous *Dayton Men's Room Address*, which many scholars rank right up there with the Gettysburg Address and The Tortoise Briefcase Address I had delivered in Kansas City. Mr. Biggshotte smiled warmly, put his arm around my shoulder (without first washing his hands!), and said, "Listen, Arnold Apathy is holding up some of the funds for a few months pending my performance of certain conditions in the sale agreement. On top of that, the insurance company hit me with a surprise transfer fee this morning, so there isn't a dime left to give you today. But as soon as we work out the other items, I'll have enough to pay you." Mr. Biggshotte had given new meaning to the word *gall*, considering the fact that, by his own admission, it was *I* who had saved him with the insurance company, and that had I not done so there would not have been a closing!

He then looked me in the eye—as his smile broadened into a toothy grin reminiscent of the Big Bad Wolf in his infamous verbal exchanges with Little Red Riding Hood—and said warmly, "Don't worry, I'll take care of you (heh, heh)."

On numerous occasions, in the months following the closing, Mr. Biggshotte reiterated to me that I had done a fantastic job of selling his property and, in particular, saving him from the clutches of the insurance company. To his credit, he repeatedly told me that I had more than earned my full commission. Notwithstanding his ongoing praise and admissions, however,

"Don't worry, I'll take care of you (heh, heh)."

he pointed out the facts of life—that because he had terrible financial problems, he could only offer me two alternatives: I could either wait until he "straightened himself out financially" (whatever that was supposed to mean) or I could file a lawsuit against him (in which case, he said, he would resort to every dirty trick in the book in order to drag the suit out for three or four years).

P.S. At my deposition, long after I had filed suit against Mr. Biggshotte, Sam Sewage, and Eddie Enigma, I drew a great round of laughs from their attorney, the judge, the court reporter, and even Mr. Biggshotte himself when I reiterated the latter's final words to me in the men's room, and added: "The trouble is, I wasn't smart enough at the time to understand what he meant when he said he would 'take care of me.'" The judge loved it, but, unfortunately, I wasn't getting paid to entertain judges.

Ultimately, we settled the suit for $35,000. At the time, I was bitter. However, in retrospect, considering the Jungle characters with whom I was dealing, I think I was very lucky to end up getting even a third of my chips.

Why had I agreed to the $35,000 compromise?

First, Eddie Enigma had declared bankruptcy shortly after the closing, so I had no recourse against him. Second, it turned out that there was a clause in the limited-partnership agreement that, *contrary* to what Mr. Biggshotte had assured me, specifically *prevented* him from entering into a contract for the sale of the Dayton property without Sam Sewage's approval. It went without saying that Sam Sewage and Eddie Enigma would, on general Jungle principles, support Mr. Biggshotte in The Big Lie and claim that I had been notified of the existence of the sale-prevention clause prior to my working on the deal. Third, Sam Sewage pointed out that he had specifically refused to sign the agreement when I visited him in Washington, and, even though this was technically a moot point by virtue of his being a party to closing the sale, judges have been known to listen to irrelevancies on more than one occasion.

Each of my commission agreements always clearly spelled out that whoever signed the agreement was doing so as an individual and assuming personal responsibility for any and all commitments called for in the agreement, *regardless* of the actual owning entity. As a consequence, the only real hope I had was to go after Mr. Biggshotte, and I didn't like the prospects of collecting from him. Indications were that he had been in financial difficulty since nursery school, and, from what I could gather, things were only getting worse for him. I had to consider the possibility that if the suit dragged on much longer, Mr. Biggshotte might join many of his fellow real estate developers and go belly up. And in the event that happened, I would have spent a great deal of additional time, energy, and money, and still not have collected a penny.

I therefore decided to grab the $35,000 and chalk another noxious affair up to experience. Shame on me. I had possessed a great image, I had managed to collect all the necessary legal tools, and I had executed my duties to perfection, all to no avail. In addition, I had recognized early on that I was dealing with a classic Type Number One, so I felt I was fully prepared to handle his treachery. Nonetheless, when it came time to show my Tortoise stuff—when I reached the one yard line—I blew it. I was so busy lapping up Mr. Biggshotte's flattery that I committed an infraction on the scoring play. And that, for an experienced graduate of Screw U., is indefensible

My attorney knew better than to ask me how I felt after the Dayton closing, but, if he had, I would have replied, "Dumb."

CHAPTER 18

THE TORTOISE
RETURNS TO TRUE FORM

After the Dayton fiasco, I was determined never again to be lulled into a mental lapse when money was on the line. I vowed that in the future I would move swiftly at the first sign of trouble. In my next deal, in which both the principals and their properties were located in Memphis, I was wary from the outset, because I immediately spotted the two partners as classic Type Number Twos. There was no doubt in my mind that they were devious, and that they would try to separate me from my chips at the first opportunity to do so.

One of the partners ("Bubba"), himself an attorney, was a habitual back-slapper—always laughing, joking, and telling you what a "good ole' boy" you were—a wheeler-dealer who had little in common with the pure version of Legalman. Wheeler-dealer

195

attorneys either do not practice law at all or practice it only as a sideline, using their law certificate as a respectable front for maneuvering their way into business deals.

The other partner ("Mumbles") was an entirely different breed of Type Number Two. He simply mumbled his way incoherently through every conversation, which made it easy for an alert-again tortoise to recognize that he was not to be trusted.

What with being constantly slapped on the back and told that I was a good ole' boy by Bubba and being periodically mumbled at by Mumbles, I had all I could do to protect my flanks. I was, of course, licensed as a real estate broker in Tennessee, had a signed commission agreement with Bubba and Mumbles, and had made certain that plenty of certified mail went back and forth between my office and the principals, so I was in a strong legal position. I also had what had become my standard image factors going for me, including my flitting in and out of Memphis via private jet.

Our original commission agreement called for a purchase price of about $1.2 million over a combined first-mortgage balance of roughly $3.6 million, or a total purchase price in excess of $4.8 million. About a month after we signed the agreement, the company who had purchased both the Dayton and St. Louis properties submitted a written offer of $950,000 (over the existing mortgages) for the two apartment developments. Arnold Apathy, who had been the point man for his firm on both the Dayton and St. Louis deals, visited Memphis to inspect the properties, at which time the sellers informed him that a $950,000 offering price was too low. With that, Arnold departed Memphis, and the situation was left hanging.

In the meantime, Ernest Ego, the head of the real estate investment trust that had purchased the Kansas City properties, made an offer of $1.4 million (over the mortgages) for the Memphis apartments, but it was part cash, part stock. Trooping back to Memphis with Ernest, I succeeded in getting Bubba and Mumbles to sign a tentative agreement to sell at the $1.4 million figure. However, after Ernest and I left Memphis, Bubba and

Mumbles managed to nitpick and chisel to such an extreme that both Ernest's $1.4 million offer and Arnold Apathy's $950,000 offer evaporated.

Just about the time I was ready to throw in the towel on the Memphis deal, I was able to come up with yet a third prospective buyer, this one from Pittsburgh. I succeeded in getting one of the partners in the buying group to travel to Memphis and meet with Bubba and Mumbles. After many hours of negotiations, he returned to Pittsburgh to discuss the deal with his partners. Shortly thereafter, another one of the Pittsburgh partners came to Memphis, and he submitted a purchase contract that called for $1.075 million over the mortgages. However, the offer had a number of onerous strings attached to it, which resulted in Bubba and Mumbles turning it down. About a week later, the Pittsburgh buying group upped its offer to $1.275 million, but the terms of the new offer were even more onerous than those in the first offer.

Following the final Pittsburgh offer, Arnold Apathy stepped back into the bidding and raised his offer to $1 million. However, having witnessed how Bubba and Mumbles had a penchant for nitpicking and dragging things out, he was smart enough to attach an important condition: The offer had to be accepted within 20 days. Nonetheless, Bubba and Mumbles continued to resist, and, to my surprise, Arnold increased his bid yet again—to $1.1 million, but $200,000 of the purchase price was to be in the form of a 10-year second mortgage at the rate of 6 percent per annum.

After a few more weeks of fiddling, Bubba and Mumbles managed to play all three hands against each other so clumsily that they ended up with no offers at all. Normally, if I was lucky enough to find just one serious buyer for a property, I felt I was in great shape. But in this case, I had managed to bring no less than three buyers to Memphis, and all three had drifted away while Bubba and Mumbles continued to fiddle.

I was becoming convinced that these two boobs, either out of sheer stupidity or masochistic design, were intent on fiddling their projects right into bankruptcy. However, before officially writing the deal off as just another bad experience, the tortoise in me decided to press on and present the deal to a few more prospective buyers. Incredibly, I was able to come up with yet a fourth prospect, this one from Cleveland. Which gave me hope, because compared to Cleveland, Memphis must have looked like the French Riviera to the buyer.

Like the three previous prospects, the Cleveland buyer ("Gentleman Jim") indicated that he, too, was prepared to make a trip to Memphis. I was starting to worry that I was getting pulled into wasting still more valuable time and money by making a fourth trip to Bubba-Mumbles land. I also wondered if they weren't just getting some sort of perverse thrill out of having people make offers to them. In the end, though, persistence won out, and back to Memphis I went. And, lo and behold, after the usual ho-hum physical inspection, Gentleman Jim made a verbal offer of $1.1 cash over the mortgages.

On this trip to Memphis, however, it became clear to me that Bubba and Mumbles were in even more serious financial trouble than I had originally suspected. In fact, after Gentleman Jim and I departed Memphis, I found out that Bubba and Mumbles had made a special trip to New York in an attempt to revive Arnold Apathy's offer. In an apparent state of panic, the Memphis Muttonheads again tried to play all the prospective buyers against one another. Mumbles sent me a telegram from New York stating that he and Bubba would accept Gentleman Jim's $1.1 million offer, but only on two conditions.

The first condition—surprise!—was that I had to agree to cut my commission to $50,000. The second condition was that Gentleman Jim would have to make the $1.1 million verbal offer official by noon the next day. As I emphasized earlier, bluffing wealthy people is futile, because they have staying power. Gentleman Jim, of course, refused to be hurried into an official acknowledgement, so there was no deal.

A few days later, I received another telegram from Mumbles (who was still wandering the streets of New York trying to put together a deal) in which he informed me that he and Bubba were *unilaterally* canceling our commission agreement and that all the deals I had presented to them were officially off the table. Sure, Mumbles, whatever you say. (I've always been fascinated by unilateral proclamations that imply that the person making them has the legal authority of an emperor. Engaging in Napoleonic hallucinations is the sport of choice for real estate developers.)

In the meantime, unbeknownst to Bubba and Mumbles, I succeeded in getting Gentleman Jim to put his $1.1 million offer in writing, so I had another major decision to make: Should I stop throwing good money after bad, or was my investment in Memphis already so great that I couldn't afford not to try to put a deal together (aka "the previous investment trap")? The irresistible aroma of money won out. I decided to try one more time, but promised myself that, regardless of the outcome, this would be the last trip I would make to Memphis.

I explained to the now extremely panicked Bubba and Mumbles that Gentleman Jim was very serious about going through with a quick closing on their properties at the $1.1 million figure, and that they had better get their act together if they wanted to bail out. That's when Mumbles mysteriously and suddenly developed the ability to speak clearly. He proceeded to let me know that it had been my commission that had been the problem with each of the other deals. He went on to say that there was no way I could expect to make the $140,000 fee called for in our agreement unless I could get Gentleman Jim to come up to the original $1.2+ million asking price. (Of course, experience had taught me that even if a seller believed he would pay me my full commission if he got the price he was asking, he would *still* find a reason to argue that my commission was too high. In other words, it has less to do with selling price than with the mental illness of the seller.)

Things were getting pretty ugly, but reality was emerging. I had to make a decision. I had already made an incredible six trips to Memphis, including four trips with serious buyers, and had produced no less than four written offers. In each of the first three cases, Bubba and Mumbles had fiddled around until the offers slipped away, and I was certain that the fourth offer was also about to go south on me if something positive didn't happen very quickly. There certainly was no way I was going to get lured into making another trip to Memphis, or even submitting the properties to another prospective buyer, if Gentleman Jim's offer wasn't accepted. Similar to my Dayton deal, then, I rationalized (that terrible word again) that if I could make any commission at all on this deal, I would look at it as found money.

So, after several hours of negotiations, I agreed to lower my commission to $75,000 on a sale price of $1.1 million. We drew up a new commission agreement similar to our initial understanding, with an added clause stating that Bubba and Mumbles agreed to accept a purchase price of $1.1 million from Gentleman Jim. It also called for them to pay me a $75,000 commission if the deal was finalized.

Subsequently, Gentleman Jim formalized his $1.1 million offer, and we began working toward a closing. As we neared the closing, however, both my attorney and I began having difficulty getting either Bubba or Mumbles on the phone—a sure sign that storm clouds were starting to gather. Finally, on the Friday before the first closing (the sale was to take place in two stages, because the second of the two properties was not yet completed), my attorney and I managed to get through to Bubba.

He was his good old, jovial self, spewing out a nonstop series of good-'ole-boy lines. He assured us that, as far as he knew, "everything was all set" and he "didn't foresee any problems" with my commission. By then, however, it was easy for me to translate his assurances into meaning that I was about to become the victim of another commissiondectomy if I didn't move fast. It was sort of like an NFL owner assuring the media that he has no intentions of firing his head coach—which, of course, really means that the coach is on the verge of unemployment.

Given that Bubba was an attorney and that my attorney had already had several discussions both with Bubba and the attorney representing him and Mumbles in the sale of their properties, I thought it would be a good idea to rely totally on the Universal Attorney-to-Attorney Respect Rule. In a strategic move, I decided to send my attorney to the Memphis closing *alone*, figuring that my presence would just serve as an irritating reminder to Bubba and Mumbles that I actually had to be paid a commission. I figured that my attorney should have no problem dealing with his counterpart in Memphis, given that the Universal Attorney-to-Attorney Respect Rule was honored throughout the world.

At the closing, my attorney presented a copy of my signed commission agreement to Legalman, as well as to a representative of the title company handling the transaction. Legalman then asked my attorney if he would please wait in the reception room so the buyer and sellers could talk in private. No problem. They then proceeded to give a whole new meaning to two words: *gall* and *crooked*. Unbelievably, all the parties worked in concert to close the deal while *my* attorney sat trustingly by himself in the reception room!

Gentleman Jim, though sympathetic to my position, followed the Arnold Apathy line and pleaded buyer impotence—i.e., the matter of my commission was between the sellers and me. To his credit, he did insist that my name be inserted in the purchase agreement as the broker of record. However, the agreement also made it clear that it was the sellers' responsibility to pay my commission, so, giving Gentleman Jim the benefit of the doubt, he may have naively assumed that it would be paid right after the closing.

If so, he was wrong. My attorney, much like The Tortoise in the Dayton deal, had been caught sucking his thumb in the reception room while the chips were changing hands behind closed doors. I had never considered the possibility of Legalman ignoring the sacred Universal Attorney-to-Attorney Respect Rule and blatantly deceiving a fellow attorney.

When my attorney called me from Memphis and relayed the bad news, I remember thinking to myself that no matter how careful I was, it was impossible to cover every conceivable way that a seller could think of to prevent me from collecting my chips. At this point, there was no question in my mind that the only limit to crookedness was a serial crook's creativity, and real estate developers in particular tend to be very creative.

The coup de grace came the day after the Memphis closing when I received a certified letter from Bubba's and Mumbles' attorney proclaiming that our commission agreement was terminated for "breach" on my part, and that it was completely null and void. (Yep, another Napoleonic proclamation.) It was obviously an absurd letter, but it was quite a learning experience. The letter was dated the day after Bubba had assured me and my attorney over the phone that "everything was all set." It was postmarked Sunday (the day after it was written), making it obvious that the sellers had intended for it to arrive subsequent to the closing on Monday.

In other words, while Bubba had been telling my lawyer over the phone that he "didn't foresee any problems" with my commission, he and Mumbles had already been planning to send me a letter claiming that I wasn't entitled to any commission at all. Then, at the closing, Bubba, Mumbles, and Legalman had eased my attorney out of the room and hurried through the proceedings before he could figure out what was happening. We're not talking about Jungle creatures here; we're talking Jungle *lice*. There's a pretty ugly difference between the two.

I had been through many repugnant situations—both during and after my days at Screw U.—but I had never seen anything quite like the shenanigans that were resorted to in Memphis. When it came to out-and-out, diabolical plotting in an effort to defraud, Bubba and Mumbles were in a class by themselves. I wasn't shocked that the principals were trying to cheat me out of my commission; that's par for the course in the real estate brokerage business. I was just awed by the extent to which these two felonious and foul organisms were willing to go to accomplish their objective.

Because the Universal Attorney-to-Attorney Respect Rule had been violated, my attorney took the matter personally. He sent Bubba's and Mumbles' attorney a letter in which he stated, among other things, that the letter he had sent to me on the eve of the closing was unfounded and ridiculous, not to mention that it was far too late. In addition, my attorney admonished Legalman for communicating directly with me when he was well aware that I was represented by an attorney. What's the world coming to when you can't depend on the Universal Attorney-to-Attorney Respect Rule? The next step is all-out anarchy.

It was my good fortune, however, that the sale of the smaller of the two Memphis properties had yet to be closed, and that the second closing could not occur until all construction and occupancy requirements were met. My attorney and I hired a bright young trial lawyer in Memphis to intervene before the second closing, and he proved to be aggressive and tough. He was successful in obtaining an attachment against the property involved in the second closing, for which I had to put up a bond.

Unlike Dayton, I had moved swiftly, and, aided by a bit of luck, managed to avert a total catastrophe. I was able to salvage my reduced commission as a result of having the those three, all-important legal tools in my bag: (1) a real estate license in the state where the properties were located, (2) a signed commission agreement, and (3) plenty of certified mail in my files.

In addition to suing Bubba and Mumbles, I also sued the title company. About a week after the suit was filed, I wrote a letter to the president of the title company in which I stated that I thought it was shameful that his firm would be a party to such blatant deception. I again put him on notice about the commission agreement that existed between the sellers and me, and enclosed another copy of the agreement. I also told him that I was holding him personally responsible for seeing to it that my commission was paid at the second closing. Obviously, however, he didn't give a hoot what a shell-shocked real estate broker thought, because my commission was *not* paid at the second closing.

The only thing that saved me was a court order that held up the proceeds of the sale. Shortly after the year in which I closed the Memphis deal, Bubba and Mumbles, undoubtedly out of financial desperation, made a $50,000 settlement offer. My Memphis attorney encouraged me not to be in any hurry to accept the offer, and I probably should have listened to him. However, the day before the first depositions were scheduled to be taken, I decided to accept it.

Why? Again, I had examined the downside closely, and pragmatism prevailed. Bubba and Mumbles, like so many other real estate developers with whom I had dealt, were in shaky financial condition, to put it mildly, and I had to consider the possibility of both of them ending up in bankruptcy court. And if that were to occur, I probably would not be able to collect anything at all. I also had to consider the fact that the party in the wrong always has an advantage, that being the fact that the wheels of justice turn very slowly. In the meantime, the person in the right has to spend thousands of dollars in legal fees, travel expenses, and other related costs. I had no choice but to face the reality that even if I won in court, I would likely net much less than the $50,000 being offered. Welcome to the Jungle, Mr. T ... again.

The Memphis tale of deceit is a perfect example of why I have emphasized that the main purpose of real estate licenses, brokerage agreements, and certified mail is to *avoid* lawsuits. If the person you're dealing with decides to go for your chips, notwithstanding his knowledge of the legal tools you have in your bag, the reality is that you probably are still going to end up losing. At the very least, you will net a lot less than you would have made had it not been necessary to litigate. Bottom line: You either win on the Jungle playing field or you're unlikely to win at all.

The Memphis deal also reaffirmed the fact that sellers—particularly Type Number Twos—will go to virtually any extreme to avoid paying a commission. In addition, it again reminded me that—like insurance companies—banks, title companies, and other institutions have built their corporate empires on human blood, and that I should not allow myself to be lulled into a false sense of security just because big firms are involved in a sale.

Finally, it put me on guard to the reality that Legalman was quite capable of participating in a devious plot against a fellow attorney in an effort to do me out of my commission. Granted, this was an unusual role for Legalman, as he normally abides by the Universal Attorney-to-Attorney Respect Rule and just plays good, hard-nosed defense, but it was yet another Jungle danger to be on the alert for in the future.

Everything considered, the Memphis outcome was a plus. I had spotted Bubba and Mumbles as Type Number Twos from the outset, and had just played along with their phony act. I also had not only secured all the necessary legal tools, but, as was not the case in Dayton, once the sellers had begun to swing their axe, I pulled my hand away and took swift action. True, Bubba and Mumbles did manage to nip off the ends of a couple of my fingers, but at least I had been quick enough to walk away with sufficient chips to be able to afford a new paint job on my badly scarred shell.

CHAPTER 19

THE ULTIMATE INSURANCE POLICY

My Dallas closing—the sale of two apartment developments totaling approximately 340 units—served as a
model for implementing my reality-based philosophy.
It was quick, clean, free of anxiety, and there were no last-minute
hitches.

Two factors, in particular, were especially significant in this
deal. First, I used my strong posture to persuade the seller to sign
a commission agreement based on 5.5 percent of the total selling
price rather than the 3 percent figure I normally used. After my
Dayton and Memphis experiences, I took it as an article of faith
that every seller worth his salt would, at a minimum, try to at
least whittle down my commission—*regardless* of what figure
we had agreed to.

That being the case, I thought it would be interesting to see if starting out at a higher commission figure than I hoped to actually receive would produce better results. When the inevitable commissiondectomy attempt began, I would be able to better afford to have my commission cut. It was just a matter pacifying the seller's sick mind. My experience had convinced me that the important thing for him was to believe that he had succeeded in shafting the real estate broker who had committed the dastardly sin of selling his property for him (and probably saving his financial hide in the process), even if his belief was an illusion.

In this deal, the seller ("Paul Pervertte") lived in San Antonio, but commuted regularly to Dallas. My image was strong from the outset, and I developed an unusually good rapport with him. Shuffling Paul back and forth between Dallas and San Antonio on my Learjet didn't do anything to hurt my image or rapport with him, either. Just a year earlier, I may not have been able to get Paul to even sign a commission agreement. Now, with my Earth brochure, Learjet, and the addition of one other factor—a track record of having closed a number of verifiable, major deals—I not only was able to get Paul to sign an agreement, but one that called for a commission percentage nearly double that called for in my previous agreements. In fact, it was about twenty-five times greater than the percentage I had received in the St. Louis Massacre just a few years earlier. I was very conscious of the fact that it was not what I was saying and doing that made the difference in my ability to steer and control the situation; rather, it was my posture.

Since our agreement contained an asking price of nearly $3 million, my commission was officially slated to be about $165,000. However, I always kept in mind that what I was actually shooting for was a commission in the area of $90,000 (based on 3 percent of the asking price). Further, I realized that if I was fortunate enough to conclude a sale, the final selling price, as in all sales, would undoubtedly be considerably less than the original asking price.

Sure enough, when money finally changed hands, the price was closer to $2.7 million. (Technically, it was less than $1.7 million, because the buyer actually purchased only a one-half interest in the properties, then leased his half back to the seller.) My commission ended up being $100,000, or nearly 4 percent of the final purchase price and more than 6 percent of the full purchase price (i.e., the total value of the property based on the one-half purchase price). As a result, by starting out with a higher commission rate in my "written understanding," I was able to walk away with about $20,000 more than I would have made under my standard 3 percent formula.

The second significant factor in the Dallas closing was that I had an additional insurance policy going for me to make certain that I got paid. As usual, in addition to my commission agreement, I possessed the other two essential legal tools: a brokerage license in the state of Texas and plenty of certified mail going from me to the principals. More important, however, was the fact that I was dealing with a buyer ("Manny Moral") who was willing to break the apathy barrier and insist that paying my commission be a condition of the closing. (The buyer was actually a real estate investment trust of which Manny was the president.)

There were many reasons why I enjoyed such strong support from Manny, but I believe the most important one was that he had the foresight to realize that it was to his advantage to see to it that I was treated fairly. Even though I had never completed a sale with Manny, I had submitted many presentations to him, and, being a major buyer of properties, he was savvy enough to recognize that my work was very professional and that I could be an excellent source of properties for his trust. He had often indicated how impressed he was with the thoroughness and accuracy of my presentations, and he appreciated my promptness in following up whenever he showed an interest in a property.

It was an ideal situation, one that reminded me very much of the association I had enjoyed with my elderly Type Number One professor at Screw U. when I was in the second-mortgage business. I was beginning to see how the buyer-support factor could be powerful enough to offset even a lack of one or more of the essential legal tools in the event I was unable to acquire them.

I had come 180 degrees from the point where I had been just a few years earlier. In the Dallas deal, I had every exit covered. Paul Pervertte had nowhere to turn, and, as a result, did not even attempt a commissiondectomy—which was a first. In fact, things went so smoothly that I was never even sure whether Paul was a Type Number One or Type Number Two. And it really didn't matter, because by gaining the buyer's full support I removed all temptation from the seller's grasp. Helping Paul Pervertte avoid sin was one of the most humanitarian acts I have ever performed.

Also, since Paul was in the usual seller's financial bind, I was able to extract excellent cooperation from Legalman. As a result, the closing went more smoothly than I ever could have imagined. It was by far the quickest sale I had ever made, with less than three months elapsing between the time my commission agreement was signed and the actual closing.

Though it was obvious to me that I had Manny's full support, I nonetheless brought my attorney along to the closing. Manny had assured me that it wasn't necessary, but I was glad that I did, because it also gave my attorney the opportunity to develop a good relationship with Manny, which in turn made future closings even easier to handle. After all the papers had been signed and the closing was wrapped up, I left Dallas to tend to another deal while my attorney stayed behind to collect my fee. And this time, he did. What a difference a good relationship with the seller had made, and what a difference a good posture had made in enhancing that relationship.

When my attorney remitted the commission check to me, he enclosed a letter in which he pointed out that, because of some of the usual last-minute contingencies, Manny's attorney had wanted to escrow $100,000 from Paul's proceeds and $25,000 from my commission. Manny, however, had insisted that none of my money be held back. My attorney closed the letter by saying, "... [this] indicates to me that he (Manny) certainly thinks a good deal of you." That statement summed up my current posture in a nutshell. Although I couldn't count on having such a great insurance policy in every future closing, in the Dallas deal I felt I had achieved the optimum posture for a real estate broker.

Not very exciting to write about, but I only wish that all my previous closings, as well as the scores of deals that didn't close, had been as unexciting as Dallas. Of course, had that been the case, I would not have had the material to write this book. What creates excitement is problems—excitement you don't want if you're looking to be paid a commission. In Dallas, I had pulled $100,000 worth of chips off the table without getting so much as a manicure from the seller.

As a result of this unique experience, it was now clear to me that the easiest way to win against intimidating sellers was to put a great deal of effort into forming good relationships with serious buyers.

CHAPTER 20

STICKING WITH A WINNING FORMULA

My next closing, in Omaha, followed quickly on the heels of my Dallas success. This time around, I wasn't able to negotiate an agreement with the higher-than-usual commission rate I had secured in the Dallas deal, but I was again working with Manny Moral, so I felt secure. In addition to having the support of the buyer, there were three other significant factors in the Omaha deal that are worth noting.

First, it was a complicated sale, not only because there were fifteen properties involved, but also because it was structured similar to the Dallas deal; i.e., it was technically a purchase of a one-half interest in the properties on a sale-leaseback basis. The deal called for Manny's company to pay $1.3 million for a 50 percent interest in the properties, then lease its half back to the seller ("Scott Scamm").

The second significant factor in Omaha was that even though the sale price was technically only about one-half of the original asking price, and even though my commission agreement called for only 3 percent of the total selling price, I was able to get paid on the basis of a 100 percent sale rather than the 50 percent sale that was technically concluded. Since Scott had legally sold only a one-half interest in his fifteen properties, the real selling price was more in the area of $4.5 million rather than the $9 million+ asking price that was stated in my commission agreement. Accordingly, he could have made a good argument that my commission should be only 3 percent of approximately $4.5 million, or about $135,000. But because I had the full support of the buyer, I was able to collect a commission of $238,000. That's an additional $103,000 just for putting in the time and effort to initiate and maintain a good relationship with Manny Moral.

The result was a "reverse commission dectomy"; i.e., I received a commission that was actually *higher* than the commission that was spelled out in my agreement. It was a delicious triumph, especially considering the fact that I didn't have the advantage of having a 5.5 percent commission rate in my brokerage agreement as I did in the Dallas deal.

My rationale for insisting that my commission be based on a 100 percent sale price was that both the buyer and seller were fully aware that the sale of a one-half interest was merely a structuring convenience and that, for all practical purposes, Manny Moral's company was really buying the properties outright. Further, I had done the same amount of work as if the deal had been closed on a 100 percent-sale basis, so I saw no reason why I should be penalized as a result of structuring technicalities.

In fact, there were a number of stipulations in the purchase agreement whereby Manny's company could end up owning the other half of the properties, either through default or by purchasing them at a very low price. And, as you might have guessed, default is precisely what ended up happening.

The third significant factor in Omaha was that I ran into a new variety of Type Number Two. When you categorize people into just three types, you obviously get many subtle variations within each group. In the case of Omaha, the seller, Scott Scamm, was a "dumb as a fox" Type Number Two. He was a bear-like figure—probably 240 pounds or more—and came across as a very docile, nice guy, always scratching his head and professing to be confused. (Was it possible, I wondered, that he and Mumbles may have evolved from a common ancestral tree of horse thieves?) The dumb act is a disarming, tried-and-true gimmick that tends to relax the opposition, because the person who uses it does not pose a visible threat to his prey.

Scott also had another tool that he employed with perfection. Not only was he a huge man, and not only did he appear to be docile and confused, he also spoke with a thick Baltic accent. This was the real clincher, because—and perhaps this is a result of American arrogance—U.S. folks tend to make the mistake of assuming that someone with a foreign accent isn't all that sharp. As it turned out, though, Scott was one of the most cunning, clever people I would encounter in the real estate business. It was a great learning experience for me, and one in which I was again able to earn while I learned.

After getting Scott to sign my commission agreement, I left two of my secretaries behind in Omaha to gather the material needed to do presentations on the fifteen properties. About a month later, I registered the eventual buyer—Manny Moral's real estate investment trust—with Scott. Shortly thereafter, I flew to Milwaukee to pick up Manny in my Learjet, and we cruised down to Omaha for another one of those thrilling episodes of brick staring.

Fortunately, it was summer, so Omaha was still accessible to aircraft. During most of the winter, Omaha looks like a throwback to the Ice Age. Even Cleveland starts to sound tropical if you spend too much time in Omaha in the winter. So, taking advantage of the nice weather, I suggested that Manny, Scott, and I view the fifteen properties from my Learjet.

If you've never flown on a Learjet, there's no way you can appreciate how ill-advised my suggestion turned out to be. The inside of a Learjet is about the size of a coffin. If you're over ten years of age, there's no way you can stand up in a Learjet. About the only movement it was intended to allow for is scratching your ear.

Nonetheless, there we were, buzzing over Omaha at an altitude of just a few hundred feet, with the massive, 240-pound Scott Scamm—comically reminding me of Br'er Bear—hurling himself from one side of the plane to the other and shouting, in his thick Baltic accent, that we were just coming over ... no, we were just going over ... no, we had just *passed over* another one of his properties. Just about the time Manny or I would be getting to the window through which he was pointing, Scott would be lunging to the other side of the plane, usually resulting in a "shall we dance" type of collision situation on our knees. It's a wonder the plane didn't roll over. I darn near cracked my shell getting slammed around between Br'er Bear and the sides of my flying coffin.

After we landed, Manny and I, bruised and battered, continued our tour of the fifteen properties on the ground. That, however, turned out to be an even worse experience. Scott drove us from project to project, and the ride was more frightening than our Learjet tour had been. (That night, I had a nightmare that I was driving in heavy traffic in a small town in Lithuania, and all the other cars on the road were being driven by Scott Scamm clones. Nothing short of terrifying.)

After the normal back-and-forth hassling, including a courageous goal line stand by Legalman, we managed to get the deal closed on the 50 percent sale-leaseback basis. Having had proof in Dallas that I had Manny's full support, I did not even bother to attend the closing. Instead, I had my attorney collect

"Du . . . vee jus paz over annuder vun of mine properties."

the $238,000 commission check for me while I was off working on other deals.

I could not help but recall how just a few years earlier I had startled everyone in that first deal in Cincinnati by showing up at the closing with my attorney. Now, working from a position of strength—which included the full support of the buyer—not only was it taken for granted that my attorney would be at the closing, it was not even necessary for *me* to take the time to be there.

Omaha was the last sale I closed during the first twelve-month period in which I implemented my reality-based philosophy, and it was a perfect note on which to end my year's work. By this time, the Earth brochure, the Learjet, and a track record of many major closings had become my trademarks. Groveling around on my hands and knees for bones now seemed a distant nightmare to me. In Omaha, I had again proven to myself, beyond a shadow of a doubt, that it wasn't what a person said or did that mattered, but what his posture was when he said or did it.

Understanding the reality of the Theory of Intimidation and the Posture Theory had led me to the ultimate in real estate brokerage: the performance of a "reverse commissiondectomy." I love you, Manny.

CHAPTER 21

ANSWER: *NOT* TO BE INTIMIDATED

Displayed on the following page is a summary chart of the deals I've described in the previous six chapters. Though all of these sales were closed during the first year following the implementation of my reality-based philosophy, it's important to understand that they represent only a small fraction of the total number of deals I worked on during that time period. As everyone who has had any experience in selling knows, the law of averages is a salesman's best friend. No matter how good you are, you will only close a small percentage of the sales you work on. It therefore logically follows that having as many deals in the hopper as possible will directly affect the number of sales you close.

Without an understanding of the Theory of Next, it's unlikely that I would have closed even one of the deals listed

City	Description of Real Estate	Approximate Sale Price	Gross Commission Received
Kansas City #1	4 apartment developments	$ 6,500,000	$221,446.50
Kansas City #2	4 apartment developments	6,000,000	205,454.89
Dayton	1 apartment development	4,000,000	35,000.00
Memphis	2 apartment developments	4,500,000	50,000.00
Dallas	2 apartment developments	1,600,000*	100,000.00
Omaha	15 apartment developments	4,500,000*	238,000.00
		$27,100,000	$849,901.39

*The actual values of the Dallas and Omaha properties were closer to $2,700,000 and $7,700,000, respectively. However, only one-half of the mortgage balances were used in calculating the sales prices, because the buyer originally purchased only a one-half interest in these properties. Based on the higher values, the approximate total of all sales was $31,400,000.

in this chart. The disappointment and frustration I endured in working on the scores of properties that did not close would have totally discouraged me had it not been for my understanding of the reality that most deals do not close because of factors beyond the salesman's or entrepreneur's control.

In other words, I came to view bad endings as nothing more than temporary setbacks, as a normal part of the game. One of the most important words when it comes to mental-health maintenance is "next." It doesn't matter whether you've been shafted in a business deal or jilted by a sweetheart, developing the mental toughness to say to yourself, "Next!" will give you a new outlook on life. Given that so many things in most people's lives have a habit of not working out as planned, I believe that one of the most important keys to happiness is having the ability to quickly move on.

Once I had developed my reality-based philosophy, I realized that my success or failure would rest more on the implementation of the Theory of Reality than on any other factor. (*Reality is neither the way you wish things to be nor the way they appear to be, but the way they actually are. Either you acknowledge reality and use it to your benefit, or it will automatically work against you.*) This is the theory that proved to be the foundation for the rest of my philosophy. Without it, all my other theories combined would not have given me the results I obtained, nor could the perfect implementation of the operational techniques I developed have led to success. The failure to recognize and acknowledge reality is a lethal problem, because you cannot take the right action(s) unless you correctly perceive the facts first.

It was my relentless pursuit of reality—my determination to recognize and acknowledge truth no matter how unpleasant it might be for me to do so—that was most responsible for my being able to turn the tables on the intimidators who coveted my chips. Only after I had correctly analyzed the brutal nature of the Business World Jungle was I able to structure a workable, reality-based philosophy and the right strategies for putting that philosophy into action. This is what allowed me to benefit from reality rather than allowing it to work against me.

As a natural consequence of my reality-based philosophy, all my techniques were directly or indirectly aimed at the most important reality of all: No matter how well I performed my job, no matter how many deals I closed, the bottom line was *getting paid*. It was reality that had led me to this fifth step of what I had always heard described as "the *four* steps of selling." One last time, in honor of all those brave, fallen comrades—real estate agents who lost their dignity, their fingers, and, in some cases, their entire hands on the battlefields of far-off enemy strongholds like Omaha, Dayton, Memphis, and St. Louis: Closing deals is not the name of the game; it's only a means to an end. Your exit strategy *must focus on walking away with chips in your hand*. In every area of life—whether business or personal—getting paid is the bottom line. If you think this applies only to real estate brokerage, sorry, but you missed the book. In that event, return to page one immediately and start reading again—more slowly this time around.

Like most people I had known over the years, I had often been guilty of ignoring the realities of the Business World Jungle because I had difficulty accepting their brutal nature. What I finally came to realize, however, was that whether or not I accepted them did not change the fact that they existed. It wasn't until I forced myself to stop being an ostrich and acknowledge reality that I was able to start making serious headway in the Jungle. Relative to many of the sophomoric rules taught in numerous how-to and success books, the realities of the Jungle may seem brutal; relative to the devastating consequences that are likely to result from following such naïve prose, however, the realities of the Jungle don't seem all that bad.

When I look back on Jungle characters like my Type Number Three professor in my first deal in Cincinnati, Mr. Bigshotte in Dayton, Bubba and Mumbles in Memphis, and Scott Scamm in Omaha, I can't help but experience a warm feeling of nostalgia.

What the heck, they were just taking their best intimidation shots at me, which is how indigenous creatures establish their place on the Jungle food chain. It's all part of the game.

Me? I just keep reminding myself of the Ice-Ball Theory and try to remember that business is just a game within the bigger game of life. And when you're playing a game, it's amateurish to be mad at your opponent just because he outwits you. I guess I still have a perverse admiration for all those Type Number Ones, Twos, and Threes who made so many big plays against me. All they were trying to do was win by the rules of the game. It's just that the game happens to be played in a jungle—the Business World Jungle—and the rules are pretty loose.

On the other hand, just because you admire an opponent's ability doesn't mean you should help him get more of your chips. Believe me, Jungle creatures love it when someone is ignorant enough to give them help, but they certainly don't expect it. On the contrary, they assume you will always do what's in *your* best interest, so why disappoint them?

Unfortunately, one of the realities of the Business World Jungle is that no matter how well you do your job, you don't necessarily get what you deserve. If you think otherwise, you may well end up turning into a cobweb-covered skeleton waiting for your commission check to arrive. Remember, looking out for your own interests does not conflict with doing a good job for the person who is supposed to pay you. All you're doing is help-ing him to not "forget" about *your* cut. Regardless of what some Jungle predators would like you to believe, you *do* have a right to be fully compensated for your services, so never allow a master intimidator to con you into thinking otherwise.

Nor should you harbor contempt for Legalman. You must understand that he is not singling you out when he kills your deal. If there's one thing Legalman is not, it's prejudiced. He doesn't discriminate when it comes to killing deals. Though it may not seem like it when it's your deal he has in his crosshairs, the truth of the matter is that he's just as happy to kill the next guy's deal as yours. So if Legalman should be successful in stopping you on downs at the one-yard line, be a good sport about it and give him his due credit—but, for goodness sakes, be sure to develop a strategy for neutralizing him in your next encounter.

PEOPLE HAVE OFTEN ASKED ME HOW THEY CAN TELL WHETHER OR NOT THEY ARE PROPERLY COPING WITH INTIMIDATION. To help each reader determine the answer to this question for himself, I have designed the following test. (I am honored to tell you that the board of regents at Screw U. is seriously considering adopting this test as part of the school's curriculum.)

HOW WELL ARE YOU HANDLING THE INTIMIDATORS IN YOUR LIFE?

1. Do you often get invited to dinner, only to discover that you're the first course on the menu?

2. Do you ask Legalman's permission before going to the rest-room?

3. Are you working longer and harder hours, but just getting older?

4. Are you in awe of people who wear white hats?

5. Do you often ask your mirror:

   Mirror, mirror
   On the wall,
   Who has the most positive attitude
   Of them all?

   ... only to have your mirror answer back: "What kind of crap is this?"

6. Do you find yourself panting whenever a Court Holder enters the room?

7. Do you often wake up in reception rooms only to find that you've been sucking your thumb and playing with your yo-yo?

8. Did you go to the last costume ball dressed as a hare?

9. Do you walk around feeling secure because so many people have told you, "Don't worry, I'll take care of you?"

10. Have you noticed your fingers getting shorter and shorter each year?

11. When your house went up in flames and the firemen came crashing through to save you, were you sitting in your favorite armchair calmly playing the fiddle?

12. Do you become easily infatuated when someone tells you what a great job you're doing?

13. Do you find yourself bluffing more but walking away with less?

14. When you were a little boy, did you always want to grow up to be a good ole' boy?

15. Do you bark a lot at closings?

> **Grading Scale:** If you answered either *yes* or *no* to any of the above questions, you flunked. Why? Because it was a trick test. I just wanted to see how seriously you take yourself. My hope is that, at the very least, I succeeded in this book in getting you to think about the Ice-Ball Theory. No matter what your feeling is about the rest of my philosophy, you salvaged something from these pages if you can accept the reality that nothing you do is going to matter 50 billion years from now anyway. (In fact, with all due respect, it's probably not going to matter much *fifty* years from now.) So relax ... chill ... don't take yourself so seriously. And, above all, remember: It's just a game.

Oops! Gotta be running along now; just saw an opening to the left of some hare out there in the Jungle. Have to keep moving while he's still daydreaming. Maybe I'll be seeing you around the Business World Jungle from time to time, and perhaps we can reminisce about our undergraduate days at Screw U. and trade Legalman stories.

*"Gotta go now. Maybe I'll be seeing you
around the Jungle from time to time."*

Robert Ringer is an American icon whose insights into life have helped more people transform their aspirations and goals into reality than perhaps any other author in history. For more than three decades, his works have stood alone as the gospel when it comes to conveying worldly wisdom to millions of readers worldwide.

He is the author of two *New York Times* #1 bestsellers, both of which have been listed by *The New York Times* among the 15 bestselling motivational books of all time. He is also the publisher of RobertRinger.com, where he combines philosophy, reality, and action in his trademark style that translates into tangible results for his readers.

Ringer has appeared on numerous national television and radio shows, including *The Tonight Show, Today, The Dennis Miller Show, Good Morning America, ABC Nightline, The Charlie Rose Show,* and has made a variety of appearances on Fox News and Fox Business.

He has also been the subject of feature articles in such major publications as *Time, People, The Wall Street Journal, Fortune, Barron's,* and *The New York Times*.

To learn about Robert Ringer's life-changing new program, *Fast Track to Dealmaking Fortunes,* visit www. http://robertringer. com/products/fast-track-to-dealmaking-fortunes/